A Champion

Naomi Griffin

TEACH Services, Inc.
P U B L I S H I N G
www.TEACHServices.com • (800) 367-1844

Copyright © 2014 Naomi Griffin
Copyright © 2014 TEACH Services, Inc.
ISBN-13: 978-1-4796-0326-8 (Paperback)
ISBN-13: 978-1-4796-0327-5 (ePub)
ISBN-13: 978-1-4796-0328-2 (Mobi)
Library of Congress Control Number: 2014934576

Published by

TEACH Services, Inc.
PUBLISHING
www.TEACHServices.com • (800) 367-1844

Dedication

~~~~~~~~~~~~~~~~~

I want to dedicate this book, first and foremost, to my Lord and Savior, Jesus Christ who has blessed me abundantly throughout my life.

I also wish to dedicate this story to Daddy, Mommy, Sarah, Joseph, Jamie, Hannah, and Lydia. Thank you for putting up with all my animals and monkey business as I grew up and learned important lessons of love, patience, and forgiveness.

To Jamie, my loving husband, who happily drew the illustrations and always encouraged me and gave me helpful advice.

To Hannah and Lydia, my dear daughters, I hope you will enjoy these stories, and I pray that someday you, too, will have many stories of your own of how God has blessed and led you.

Table of Contents

Chapter 1

A Girl's Answered Prayer

~~~~~~~~~~~~~~~~~~~~

Eleven-year-old Naomi dug her toes into the dust as she gazed into the field. *4-H was fun today*, she thought as she began walking through the tall grass. *I sure like playing with dogs. I wish Tillie was my dog so we could do everything together.*

Naomi smiled as she thought of the stubborn, spunky Scottish terrier. *She's a nice dog, but she's not really my dog. If I had a dog, I would want a big dog, like Joseph's dog, one that would follow me everywhere.*

Trying to brush the thought aside, Naomi lay down in the sweet grass and watched the clouds play tag with themselves in the sky. A bumblebee hummed to himself as he searched for wildflowers. *I wonder if I really could have my own dog*, Naomi mused as she picked a flower and held it in the path of the bumblebee. The little hummer landed briefly on the flower she held in her fingers then buzzed off in search of more nectar.

After a few minutes, Naomi jumped to her feet and raced to her favorite climbing tree. Soon she was seated on a strong limb that gave her a good view of the field. As she situated herself in the tree, her mind returned to her earlier thoughts.

My rabbits and cats have been nice, but they don't really want to play with me. If I had a dog, I know it would want to play with me! We could play ball and hide-and-seek. And we could go to 4-H! We would work hard at 4-H and learn all we could together! I would want a girl, because she would understand me better. I would teach her lots of tricks, and she would be the smartest dog around!

Leaning against the tree, Naomi closed her eyes and smiled as she let her thoughts run wild as to the kind of dog she would want. She thought of the dogs in the neighborhood. There was old Lucy, the golden retriever mix, and then there was the dachshund across the street. *I would want something different,* she thought. Suddenly an idea struck her and she sat up so quickly that she almost lost her balance on the limb. "A collie!" she said out loud. "That's what I want—a sable collie like Lassie!"

Closing her eyes again she prayed, *Dear Jesus, You know what I have been thinking right now. You know how much I want a dog of my own. If is Your will, please send me the right dog. I promise to take good care of it! Thank you, amen.*

Sliding down from the tree, Naomi headed home. *I know I can trust Jesus. He knows what I need and want!* With that thought in mind, Naomi ran toward the house. If she hurried she would have time to check on her rabbits before supper.

That evening as she was getting ready for bed, she asked her mom how much a collie cost. "Quite a bit of money, I suppose. Why do you ask?" her mom said, only mildly surprised.

Naomi nervously began unbraiding her hair. "Well,"

she said, "I've been thinking a lot about collies lately ... actually about getting a dog of my own." Seeing a smile on her mom's face, she quickly added, "PLEASE, could I have my own dog? I would take good care of her! Tillie has been fun to work with in 4-H, but she isn't my dog, and you know she can be stubborn at times! And since you are thinking of breeding her soon, I won't be able to practice with her as much when she has the pups!"

Naomi let out a big sigh, relieved to be able to tell someone what she had been thinking about all day. Her mom reached for the hairbrush and began brushing Naomi's hair. "A dog is a big responsibility, Naomi. Are you sure you are ready for such a big job? Not only would you need to train the puppy, but you would need to feed her and make sure she is taken care of at night."

Naomi nodded her head, "Mommy, I would take good care of a puppy. I just want my own dog so badly; one that can go with me everywhere!"

Naomi's mom smiled again and gave her a kiss good night. "I need to talk to Daddy about it first. I love you. Sweet dreams!" With that, Mommy walked down the hallway.

The next week at 4-H, the leader said that Indy, her Australian Shepherd, was going to have puppies. Linda was not very happy about that since this was an unplanned litter. "If you know of anyone who would like an Australian Shepherd mix puppy, I should have a few soon," Linda announced to the group. Naomi shot a pleading look at Mommy.

On the way home, Naomi asked, "Did you hear what

Linda said? Indy is going to have puppies! Indy is such an obedient, sweet dog. Do you think she will have any girl puppies?"

"Naomi, don't get your hopes up. Daddy and I have not decided if this is the right time for you to get a dog. We do already have two dogs, and you can continue to work with Tillie on what you are learning at 4-H."

Every day after her schoolwork and chores were done, Naomi practiced the obedience lessons with Tillie. But the dog never seemed interested in learning anything. She would just sit and look around at the scenery when she was supposed to come to Naomi. Tillie always seemed bored with the whole ordeal.

One day when Naomi was done practicing, she ran to get Tillie's ball. Tillie fastened her eyes on the ball and started wagging her tail. "Tillie stay!" Naomi commanded as she slowly walked behind the lilac bush. "Tillie come!" Tillie dashed around the bush. "Good girl! Go get the ball!" Naomi threw it with all her might. "This is a lot more fun than the lessons we are supposed to practice."

Naomi grinned and then a thought came to her. *I wonder if I could use the ball to train Tillie. I know we would both have a lot more fun!* By then Tillie was back with the ball. *I wonder how a normal recall would be if I had the ball with me.* Naomi thought.

"Tillie stay!" Naomi backed slowly away, holding the ball behind her. After getting a few yards away, she called Tillie. This time, instead of just sitting there, Tillie dashed up and sat squarely in front of Naomi. "Wow! That really works! We are both having fun and learning at the same time!"

Naomi wandered into the upper field where wood was stacked in long rows so it would dry for winter use.

Tillie followed Naomi, begging her to throw the ball again. "Tillie, I have a great idea! Would you like to run along the top of the woodpile? They aren't leaning very much, and you don't weigh very much. How about it?"

Running toward one of the woodpiles, Naomi held the ball up for Tillie to follow. Without hesitation, Tillie climbed up one side, ran along the top, and down the other side. "Good girl, Tillie! Wasn't that fun?" Tillie chewed on her ball and wagged her tail again. "We could do so much together if you were my dog! But Mommy and Daddy say that you are the family's dog, and you are going to have puppies, so we really won't be able to do very much of this. You know how cranky you get when you have puppies!" Tillie slowly walked away, still chewing on the ball.

"Dear Jesus," Naomi prayed, "You know how much I want my own dog, and You know that Indie is having puppies very soon. If it is Your will, please let me get one of them. Please help me to trust You. Thank you. In Jesus' name, amen."

A few weeks later, Linda mentioned that Indy had had her puppies. There were two males and one female. As they got into the car, Naomi's mom causally said, "How would you like to go see Indy's puppies?"

"I would love too!" cried Naomi, grinning from ear to ear and bouncing up and down in her seat.

When they got to Linda's house, Linda greeted them and led them through the house to a quiet back room. Naomi's heart beat wildly when she saw the three puppies crawling around in a cozy box. At once, Naomi's eyes focused on a puppy that was brown with white on its paws, muzzle, and collar. *That one is colored just like a collie! Jesus, is this the dog You want me to have?* Naomi silently prayed.

Linda reached down into the box and picked up the very puppy that Naomi's eyes were fastened on. "Would you like to hold her?"

"It's a girl?" Naomi sputtered. "Ohhh! I can't believe it! She is so beautiful! She is so perfect!"

Linda laughed. "They are only two weeks old and look like oversized worms with hair, and you call them beautiful!"

The puppy grunted a little puppy grunt and snuggled up against Naomi's neck. Then, with a big sigh, she fell asleep. "It's as if she knows that we belong together!" Naomi smiled and carefully cradled the pup for as long as she could. Mommy held the other puppies, but Naomi was satisfied holding the little girl puppy.

Back at home, Mommy and Daddy disappeared into their bedroom to talk. It seemed to Naomi like an eternity before they came out of the room. Daddy had a twinkle in his eye, but merrily walked outside whistling a happy tune. Mommy hurried into the kitchen to fix supper, and Naomi followed her.

"Did you talk to Daddy about the puppies?" Naomi asked as she helped put the food on the table.

Mommy smiled. "Yes, I did."

"What did he say?" Naomi asked with a worried look on her face.

"Well, I can't tell you. Daddy wants you to talk to him about it first before any definite decisions are made. He wants *you* to tell him why you want a puppy."

That night as the family sat around the table, Naomi was quieter than usual. She picked at the food on her plate. At last, just as everyone was finishing the meal, she worked up her courage to ask about the puppy.

"Daddy?"

"Yes, Naomi." Daddy slowly got up from the table and carried his plate into the kitchen.

Naomi followed him with her plate. "Did you know that Indie had puppies?" Naomi blurted out.

"Who is Indy?" Daddy asked.

"Indy is Linda's Australian Shepherd. She is a wonderful dog! And one of her puppies is very cute, and it's a girl! I would really, really like to have that puppy. Would that be OK with you? I will take very good care of her; I promise!"

Daddy walked into the front room and sat down in an easy chair. Naomi stood by the big, warm woodstove, waiting for his reply.

"Naomi," Daddy said as he raised the footrest, "a dog is a big responsibility. If you get tired of the dog, it will still be there to take care of. Dogs can live a long time. Why do you want this dog?"

"I've been wanting a dog of my own for a long time, and I wanted a collie, or at least one that looked like a collie. I also want a girl. And Indy's puppy is all of these things! I want a dog that can be my own special friend. I want to teach her all sorts of things. She should be a really good farm dog, too! Please could I get her?" Naomi felt a little shaky inside. She held her breath and waited.

Daddy leaned back and closed his eyes as if he was thinking hard. "Three dogs," he mused, more to himself than to anyone. "Tillie at least is a little dog, but two big dogs?" Daddy let out a big sigh of resignation. "OK, Naomi, you may get the puppy. I know how you love animals, and I know you will take good care of it."

Naomi rushed over and gave Daddy a big hug. "Oh thank you, Daddy! Thank you so much! I'll take good care of her!" A little tear of joy squeezed out of her eye and dropped on Daddy's shirt.

"Now, young lady, if you are getting that puppy, you had better call Linda and let her know!" Daddy said teasingly.

"I'll call her right away!" Naomi bounced into the room where Mommy was. "Daddy said yes! I can get the puppy! I'm actually getting a dog of my own! My own Lassie dog! "

"I'm happy for you. Here is the phone. Call Linda and let her know which puppy you want."

Naomi shook a little as she waited for Linda to answer the phone.

"Linda! I may get the puppy! My folks said yes! I'm so happy!" Naomi was still wiping tears of joy from her face as she spoke.

"Which one do you want?" Linda asked.

"I want the girl—the one that is colored like a collie!"

"Alright, I'll save that puppy for you. I'm sure you will do very well together. Congratulations!"

Naomi felt as if she would burst as she hung up the phone.

Chapter 2

The Joy of a New Puppy

~~~~~~~~~~~~~~~~~~~~~~~~~~

The next few weeks were spent getting ready for the puppy to come home. Naomi and Mommy went to town to purchase a dog crate, some puppy food, and a food dish. Naomi carefully arranged everything so it would be just right. Later, she checked out lots of books from the library on puppy raising and training. Every evening she studied the books to try and learn all she could about puppies. It was hard to think about anything else, especially schoolwork.

At long last the day came for the new puppy to come home. Since it was such a special event, both Sarah and Joseph, her older sister and brother wanted to come along. When they got to Linda's house, Naomi was so excited she could hardly control herself. They all walked through the house and into the backyard.

"Puppies, puppies! Where are you?" Linda called.

Almost immediately a little brown-and-white puppy bounced around the corner of the house. She ran right over to the group and put her little paws up on Naomi's legs. Naomi reached down and swooped her up in her arms.

"My own puppy; you are my very own puppy! We are going to be best friends; I just know it!" After thanking Linda, the happy family and puppy got into the car. Naomi sat in the back seat with the puppy on her lap with Sarah on one side and Joseph on the other.

"Ohh! She's so soft!" Sarah said. "You are going to be a good girl, aren't you puppy?"

The puppy sat up and cocked her head as she looked Sarah in the eyes, as if she was trying to say. "Of course I will be a good puppy!"

"What are you going to name her, Naomi?" Joseph asked.

"The name I have been thinking of is Lucky. I think it is a good name, and I think that we both feel lucky to have each other. I know it isn't just luck. God is the one who gave me this wonderful puppy, but that is the only name I can think of that describes the way I feel. I feel very blessed and happy. God is so good!"

Once they got home, They all tumbled out of the car, and Naomi carefully put the puppy on the ground. Lucky looked up at Naomi and waited. The girl slowly turned and walked toward the house. Without hesitation, Lucky trotted after her at her heels.

This is my puppy, Naomi thought with pride. *I will take good care of her. She trusts me already! I will have to be a good leader for her. At last! I have a dog of my own. It just seems right to have a dog trotting at my heels. I love it!*

Naomi headed for the rabbit hutches. She wasted no time introducing Lucky to the other animals on the farm. The rabbits just sat and stared mildly at the puppy that appeared in their doorways. They were used to Naomi showing them other animals.

The cat was downright rude when she saw the puppy—her hair rose up on her back. Muttering something under her breath, she jumped quickly up on a fence post. From there she angrily glared down at the newcomer. Lucky didn't seem to be bothered by her impolite welcome. She just looked up calmly at the cat and cocked her head. After a grand tour of the farm, Naomi took her new companion to meet the other dogs.

When Tillie saw the puppy, she went into her crate and wouldn't come out. Everyone knew how much Tillie despised other dogs. It took her a long time to accept other dogs because she wanted nothing to do with them unless they were her own puppies.

Bear, on the other hand, didn't know what to do! Being almost a puppy himself, he got very excited. After the initial greeting, he bounced around Lucky, bowing to her. Lucky bowed back with her little stub tail wagging. Then she charged at Bear! A sudden look of shock came over Bear's face as if he suddenly didn't know what to do. When Lucky opened her mouth to give him a puppy bite, Bear jumped straight up in the air and hit the ground running with Lucky in hot pursuit. Although he seemed startled, this was one of Bear's favorite games. He loved being chased. He began running circles around the five-week-old puppy. Before long, Lucky was exhausted, and she flopped down on the grass. Bear ran up to her, sniffed her, backed up a few steps, and lay down. He stared at the puppy as if he expected her to explode any minute. Joseph and Naomi laughed at his funny expression.

"Don't worry, Bear. It is just an innocent little puppy!" Naomi giggled.

Bear crawled toward the puppy and stretched as far as he could until his nose touched Lucky. The puppy rolled over on her back. As Bear continued sniffing her, Lucky began to chew on his collar. The black dog quickly jumped to his feet with the puppy still hanging on to his collar. Bear looked at Joseph in desperation. Joseph picked up the puppy.

"There you go, Bear. Don't worry; this is a nice puppy. You will be good friends with her. Just don't let her bully you around!"

Mommy came to the door. "It's time for supper!" she called. "Come and get it!"

The children and dogs hurried inside. Naomi placed a blanket by the front door and attached a leash to the doorknob, which she then fastened to Lucky's collar so that she could stay out of trouble while the family ate.

"Well, Naomi, how do you like your new, little friend?" Daddy asked.

"Oh, she is wonderful! She is so smart! I can tell that already! As soon as I put her on the ground, she followed me! I know we will be best friends!"

Daddy refilled his soup bowl and reached for another muffin, "Have the other dogs met her yet?"

Naomi smiled. "Yes, Bear and Lucky are doing great. I think Bear is not quite sure what to think of the puppy yet, but with a little time, they will be good friends. Tillie acted as she normally does with other dogs. I'll have to watch her so she doesn't scare Lucky." Lucky sighed as she lay on the blanket. "I think I'll show Lucky the river after supper!" Naomi bubbled. "I think she will like that!"

Mommy laughed. "This has been a big day for Lucky. Be careful not to be too hard on her!"

After supper Naomi carried Lucky out into the upper field. The puppy was still a little sleepy from her nap. "Lucky, this is the upper field," the girl explained. "This is a good place to play hide and seek. I'm going to show you the old barn, the field, and the river! I think you will like this place. It has a lot of space to run and play. Would you like me to show you my favorite climbing tree?"

Lucky lifted her head at the question in the girl's voice and nuzzled Naomi's cheek.

"OK, I guess you do! I'm glad you want to see everything!" When they reached the tall grass, Naomi put Lucky down for a few minutes to play. As Lucky sniffed and snuffled around, Naomi laid down in the grass once more. It was a cool, overcast day; rain was in the air.

I remember when I laid down in this grass and dreamed of getting a dog. And now I have my dog, Naomi thought. Lucky stopped her sniffing and came over to Naomi and lay down next to her. Tears of happiness came to Naomi's eyes.

Closing her eyes, she prayed. *Thank you, Jesus, for answering my prayer. You have given me a wonderful gift. Help me to train this puppy the way You want me to. Teach me how to take care of her.*

Naomi sat up. The wind was blowing a little harder. "Well, doggie, we had better hurry if we are going to see the river before the rain gets here." Lucky trotted confidently at Naomi's heels as they headed down into the trees. After showing her the river, they turned to head back up the trail. Lucky was getting tired. She tried to keep up with Naomi, but her little legs begged for a rest. She stopped and lay down in the middle of the trail. Naomi turned around.

"Oh, I'm sorry Lucky! I guess I keep on forgetting how tired you must be! You have had a big day haven't you? Here, let me carry you back to the house. The rain is almost here, so I'll show you the climbing tree next time."

The rain caught up with them by the time they reached the field. "Well, Lucky, it looks as if we are going to get wet!" Naomi dashed for the house, cradling her special bundle.

That first evening was spent cuddling with Lucky, brushing Lucky, playing with Lucky, and watching Lucky. Before long it was time for bed. Naomi didn't want to put Lucky to bed; she was afraid that her dream-come-true would turn into just that, a dream. The puppy was placed in a dog crate on the back porch.

At two in the morning, Mommy gently shook Naomi awake. "Naomi, your puppy is crying. She probably needs to go outside."

Naomi sat up and rubbed her eyes. "OK," she mumbled as she shuffled out of the room.

"You need to wait until she stops crying for a moment. If you go to her while she is crying, she will learn very quickly to cry just to get attention," Mommy stated.

Naomi stood by the back door for a minute until the puppy stopped crying. Then she opened the door to the crate, picked up the puppy, and took her outside for a potty break. The puppy quickly relived herself and was put back to bed. But the next morning, bright and early, the little treasure was crying again. This time Naomi heard her. She jumped out of bed, got dressed, and ran out to the back porch to let the little dog out. "Come on, Lucky. Let's go feed the animals!"

Naomi and Lucky played together all day. When they came inside, Mommy called from the front room. "Naomi, have you washed your feet? You know how dirty they get when you run around barefoot all day!"

Naomi glanced down at her feet. They were quite dirty. "I'm going to wash them now," Naomi called back. She walked down the hallway and entered the bathroom. She lifted one foot and put it in the sink. *It is so much easier to wash them in the sink instead of the bathtub,* Naomi thought. *Mommy hasn't told me not to wash them in here, so I'm going to keep doing it.*

Just then Mommy's face appeared in the doorway. "Naomi! Please wash your feet in the bathtub! The sink is meant for washing hands, not feet!"

Naomi sighed, lifted her foot out, stuck it straight out in front of her, did a quarter turn, and hopped over to the tub. When Naomi turned on the water, Lucky came over to investigate the bathtub. She jumped up and put her front paws on the edge of the tub. "Lucky! Look at your feet! They are just as dirty as mine! You even have grass stains on your legs!" Picking up the puppy, Naomi placed her in the tub. She reached for the soap and scrubbed the puppy's legs and paws until they were sparkly white.

"Lucky, I don't understand it. Why is it more fun to clean your feet than mine?" The puppy licked Naomi's feet. "That's it! We'll swap! You lick my feet, and I'll clean your legs! Good girl!"

Lucky grew rapidly over the next few months. She always wanted to learn more things, and Naomi was always trying to teach her more. As soon as she had all her vaccinations, she began attending 4-H with the other dogs. Lucky loved 4-H. Every time they got ready to go, Lucky would wiggle all over and run back and forth from the car to Naomi as if trying to hurry her up. When they arrived, the puppy could hardly wait to get out of the car. As they went through the lessons, Naomi's heart swelled with pride. Lucky was doing exceptionally well in most of the exercises. However, when it came to the exercise in which a stranger had to come and pet Lucky as she stood still, Lucky would put her head down and slowly walk away. She didn't like strangers petting her, especially men.

One day when they were at 4-H, Linda came over to Naomi and said, "I'm worried about Lucky's shyness of people. You need to work on socializing her with other people. If you don't, you might have a bigger problem when she gets older. You need to take Lucky with you to meet people she doesn't know. Have them give her a treat. Don't force her to be petted by them, but just make it a fun experience for her. I know it might seem like a little thing now, but if this isn't worked out right now, she may be inclined to bite someone."

Naomi's eyes widened in surprise, *Lucky would never bite anyone! She is too sweet and obedient to do something that terrible!* she thought.

That evening Naomi grabbed one of her favorite books and ran out to the orchard. The day before she and Joseph had strung up a hammock a few inches from the ground. Naomi loved swinging back and forth while she looked up through the leaves of the old apple tree.

Soon she was lost in a story of wild horses and cowboys. *This is wonderful*, Naomi thought to herself. *I love times like this.* She squirmed around until she found a more comfortable position. *Now let's see, where was I...* Naomi ran her finger down the page. *Oh yes! Here I am. The white stallion just escaped with his mother...*

As she lay there reading, something bumped her. "Lucky, is that you?" In reply, two white paws and a puppy face peeked over the side of the hammock. "I'm sorry, doggie. I guess you are feeling a little left out aren't you?

Would you hold still if you were in the hammock with me?"

The girl lifted the puppy onto her stomach. "There, if you hold still, I will let you stay here, but if you fool around and squirm, then you will be put back on the ground! This thing is hard to balance sometimes!" Lucky lay down on Naomi's tummy with a happy groan. Soon Naomi was once again lost in her story. As she read she calmly stroked Lucky's fur.

"Hey! What's going on over there?"

Naomi sat up quickly. "Hi, Uncle Walt! We're just reading a book! What are you doing?"

Uncle Walt stood on the sidewalk leading to the house. Lucky growled. The hair on her back bristled.

"I just came over to give your mom some strawberries." He turned and started walking toward the house.

"Don't worry, Lucky, Uncle Walt is a nice person. He might sound mean, but if you are nice, he will be nice to you." Lucky growled again, and stared suspiciously as the man walked up the stairs to the front porch.

I guess I should ask Uncle Walt to pet Lucky and give her a treat so she will like him. I know that is what Linda told me to do, but I really don't feel like getting up. I'd rather read my book; anyway, he will only stay a minute. I'll wait until next time. Besides, Lucky really isn't mean; she is just shy when she doesn't know the person. With that thought, Naomi settled back into the hammock, and Lucky lay down for another snooze.

As the days went by, there were opportunities to socialize the puppy, but Naomi always had something else to do. It just didn't seem very important to her. Lucky was always sweet and loving to the family, so Naomi dismissed Linda's recommendation regarding getting Lucky used to strangers.

Naomi and Lucky often played with Rosie, a neighbor girl who also had a puppy. Kylie was a gray dog with black spots. Lucky and Kylie loved playing together. They would spend hours chasing and tumbling around as the girls played pioneers, hide-and-seek, or other games or went rollerblading.

One day Naomi hurried to finish her schoolwork. She wanted to play with Rosie and the dogs, but it was taking forever to finish her math problems. The numbers seemed to run together and make no sense. Fortunately, with some help from Mommy, Naomi at last completed her work. "May I go over and play with Rosie now? We want to work on our fort!"

Mommy smiled. "Yes, you may go and play for a while. But when I call you for supper, I want you to come inside right away. OK?"

Naomi nodded as she opened the door. "I'll listen really hard!" With that, she ran in the direction of Rosie's house, her braids bouncing on her shoulders. Soon she was knocking on her friend's door.

"Hi, Rosie! Do you want to come and work on our fort?"

Rosie had a serious look on her face. "Naomi, there is something we need to tell you. Can you come inside for a minute?" Rosie opened the door wide. As Naomi entered the kitchen, she saw that Rosie's mom also had a serious look on her face.

"Is something wrong? What happened?"

Rosie's mom put the brownies she had just finished mixing into the oven and then walked around the kitchen counter. "Something happened yesterday that we need to tell you about."

Naomi looked back and forth from Rosie to her mom. "What happened?" Naomi choked out.

Rosie's mom led the girls to the living room to sit down. "Yesterday evening Rosie and her dad were playing in the yard. You know he isn't here very much, and your dog doesn't know him very well."

Naomi frowned. "I don't understand what the problem is. Did Lucky get in the way?"

Rosie cleared her throat. "Lucky bit my dad."

Chapter 3

County Fair

~~~~~~~~~~~~~~~~~~~~~~~~~~

"What!" Naomi's mouth dropped open.

"I was just getting ready to call your mom and tell her about it when you came over. You'll have to watch Lucky closely from now on. We aren't angry with you, but you need to be careful that your dog doesn't hurt someone else."

Naomi's heart sank. "How did it happen?"

Rosie smiled. "It was actually kind of funny. I was playing badminton with my dad. We were quite close to each other since I'm just learning how to hit the birdie. Anyway, Lucky came trotting around the garage. When she saw my dad swinging the racket so close to me, she ran right over and bit him on the rear! He sure yelled!" Rosie chuckled again at the memory. "I know Lucky did that because she thought he was threatening me, but she still shouldn't bite people!"

Naomi nodded. "Thank you for telling me about it. And I'm terribly sorry it happened. My 4-H leader told me I needed to work more on socializing Lucky, but I have neglected it. What happened was my fault."

After that incident, Naomi was more careful to introduce Lucky to new people in the right way. She gently encouraged her to be friendly with the neighbors, including Uncle Walt. In time, Lucky and Uncle Walt became fast friends.

"The fair is almost here!" Naomi told Lucky one day. "We have only one more week to wait! The fair is so much fun! I hope you like it as much as I do! I know you will do really well. Even though you are only five months old, you have learned the exercises well."

Lucky looked up at Naomi and wagged her stub tail and smiled. Every day they practiced the obedience lessons, and Naomi carefully groomed Lucky until she shown. Joseph and Naomi went over and over the questions that the judge might ask them while in the show ring. The questions ranged from the rules and standards of 4-H to dog diseases. They were hard questions, and the children studied them faithfully. At last, the day came for the competition. Naomi and Joseph were clean, and their show clothes were pressed. The dogs were groomed so much that not a hair was out of place.

When Naomi entered the ring, she felt confident that she and Lucky would win. Visions of a big ribbon floated in her eyes. She had practiced and was sure that Lucky knew the routine. The judge was a woman with short hair. She wore a wide brimmed hat and smiled kindly at the contestants. Naomi and Lucky began their routine, stopping and starting at the judge's command. Then came the stand for exam.

"Lucky, stay!" Naomi commanded.

Lucky stood quietly until the judge walked up to stroke her. Then she cowered and slowly slunk over to Naomi for moral support. Naomi could tell that Lucky knew she had broken the rules, but Lucky just couldn't face the strange lady. Naomi's heart sank, and her eyes filled with tears. The rest of the routine was a blur. Lucky, sensing Naomi's disappointment, seemed to forget all she had learned. Naomi left the ring in tears. Mommy was waiting for her, and she opened her arms and gave Naomi a big hug.

"Don't worry, Naomi. You and Lucky did a very good job. Remember, Lucky is only five months old. She did the best she could."

Naomi wiped her eyes and looked up at her mother. "But I wanted Lucky to do perfect! She knows it all, but she just seemed to forget it when we were in the ring!" Lucky nudged Naomi's hand. Getting no reaction, she leaned up against her legs and looked up sorrowfully as Naomi cried.

Mommy continued. "Winning isn't everything. The prize is just a piece of material. If one just shows for the prize, one is missing the goal of showing. Showing a dog is an opportunity to do something new and exciting with them. It's all about making memories and improving communication with the dog. Of course, it's nice when you win, but don't let that be your main focus."

Naomi smiled and nodded. "I know you're right. I let the silly ribbon distract me from my wonderful puppy." Naomi bent down to pet her puppy. Lucky panted a happy smile. "You did your best, Lucky, and I am proud of you. I know the woman was scary. In fact, she was scary to me, too!" Naomi whispered. "Let's focus on just having fun for the rest of the fair, OK?" Lucky licked the girl's hand. "Alright, it's a deal!"

Lucky went home with a low scoring ribbon that year,

but it didn't bother Naomi. She just focused on teaching Lucky more things and improving her interaction with strangers.

Chapter 4

A Bad Habit

~~~~~~~~~~~~~~~~~~~~~~~~~

"Naomi! Naomi! Guess what? There are salmon in the creek!" Joseph said as he burst into the house. "Let's go and watch them! I already saw two great big ones fight their way up stream! They splashed water everywhere! Come on!"

Naomi grabbed her coat and raced out the door behind Joseph with Lucky at her heels.

"Naomi, why don't you wear shoes? You could run much faster if you would wear shoes!"

Naomi stuck out her chin. "I can keep up with you just fine, even when I don't wear shoes! Just watch!"

Soon the three of them had reached the banks of the creek. "Shh!" whispered Joseph. "We have to be quiet and hold still. The salmon might see or hear us if we make a bunch of noise!"

The children crouched in the bushes. Lucky pushed in next to them and looked down into the water. Suddenly a big fish came fighting its way upstream right under Lucky's nose. The dog gave a little jump backwards as if to say, "What in the world was that thing in the water that just splashed cold water all over me?" Lucky walked to the edge of the creek again and sniffed carefully. Then she waded into the water to investigate. Finding nothing, she turned and came back to shore with a puzzled look on her face.

"Don't feel too bad, Lucky," Naomi comforted. "Those fish are never very sociable. They like staying with their own kind."

Lucky wagged her short tail and shook cold water all over the children. "Oh, do you always have to do that right next to us?" Naomi cried.

Just then they heard another fish fighting its way toward them. This time the fish decided to take a little rest right next to the bank where the children and dog crouched.

"See if you can touch him, Joseph!" Naomi whispered.

Keeping his body low so as not to frighten the salmon, Joseph slowly reached into the water. Almost at once the old timer shot forward and on up the stream.

"Oh well, it was fun trying, but I guess those fish are on their toes. They have come a very long way and aren't about to be caught," Joseph said with a wry smile.

The next few weeks Joseph, Naomi, and Lucky spent a lot of time at the creek watching the fish. They tried many times to touch the fish with their hands, but the fish always left them with a shower of water. Gradually the fish began to grow tired and slow in their responses. Soon there wasn't any more live fish left to watch and admire. The children stopped visiting the creek as often. Lucky, however, continued to visit the creek with renewed interest. Often she would come home smelling like rotten fish. One day when Naomi went outside to play with Lucky, the dog came happily trotting over.

"Hey, Lucky, do you want to play with me?" Naomi asked, but as Lucky approached, Naomi smelled a horrible stench. "Oh! What is that smell?"

As Naomi sniffed the air, Lucky sat down and hung her head. "Is it YOU that smells so bad, Lucky?" Naomi asked in an accusing voice. Lucky slowly stood and sulked onto the back porch with a very guilty look on her face.

Naomi smiled. "Well, at least you admit it! Let me hose you off. It won't help your breath, but at least it will take some of the smell out of your coat!" Lucky slowly made her way off the back porch and moved toward Naomi.

As Naomi was bathing Lucky, she gave her a lecture. "You could get very sick from eating rotten fish! I'm going to have to watch you closely until I know you are OK."

Sure enough, that evening Lucky seemed uncomfortable. Her tummy was bloated, and she didn't have much interest in anything. Several times she had to go outside to throw up. Naomi sat with her all evening, petting her and trying to keep her comfortable.

The next morning the dog was a little better, but she was still a little slow moving around. And she wasn't interested in breakfast. Naomi sat next to Lucky, stroking her soft fur. The girl's eyes filled with tears.

"You poor puppy. I don't like seeing you so uncomfortable. My poor, poor puppy." Lucky whined and licked Naomi's hand. "I'll have to be more careful with you around rotten fish from now on."

Toward the afternoon, Lucky started taking more interest in what was going on around her. She even ate a little food. However, the dog didn't make the connection between her sickness and the dead fish, for she kept sneaking off to find fish.

Over the winter Lucky grew and matured into a big beautiful dog. She loved Naomi with all her heart and followed her everywhere. As the 4-H lessons continued, Lucky became more confident in the exercises. Linda became too busy with her business to continue to lead the 4-H group and a new leader was chosen to teach the children and dogs.

Jeanne was a very talented dog trainer, and she inspired the children to be disciplined and diligent in their work. Joseph and Naomi excelled with their dogs under Jeanne's instruction.

One day as Naomi practiced with Lucky at 4-H, Jeanne came over to her and said, "Naomi, you and Lucky are both doing so well. Lucky is watching you and understanding what you want from her. You make a good team. Would you like to join a harder class this summer?"

"Do you really think we could?" Naomi's eyes were wide with surprise. "Lucky didn't do very good last year at the fair. Do you think she could handle a harder class and compete against older dogs?"

Jeanne smiled. "Wasn't Lucky just a puppy at the last fair?"

"Yes, she was," Naomi replied.

"Your dog is older now and a lot more focused. Actually, I think the harder challenge would be good for both of you. We don't want you to get bored!"

"OK! If you think we are ready, then I'd love to try!"

"Good! You and Joseph are both ready to move on! This will be a good summer to advance." Jeanne turned and focused her attention on another handler and dog.

"Lucky, did you hear what Jeanne said? She wants us to challenge a harder class! We are going to have to work even harder! How about practicing another stand for exam?"

Soon, Naomi and Joseph were involved in advanced classes with their dogs and having a wonderful time.

Chapter 5

New Babies

~~~~~~~~~~~~~~~~~~~~~~

Spring was always an enjoyable time of year with its milder weather and blooming flowers. One day Mommy, Joseph, and Naomi climbed into the van and drove to a nearby farm. Both children were very excited, for they were going to look at baby goats. They had borrowed Bear's dog create and filled it with sweet smelling hay. Bear had lent it grudgingly, but Mother said they would need a soft bed to place the baby goats if they brought some home.

Soon the trio pulled up in front of an old gate. Inside the gate there were horses, goats, turkeys, dogs, and cows milling around.

"It's a good thing we're wearing boots!" Mommy exclaimed, noting the mud. After parking the car, they all piled out and opened and closed the gate. They walked to the house and knocked on the door. When no one answered, Joseph suggested that they try the barn.

"I think he is over there! See, there is a light on, and the door is slightly open!" Soon the three of them were wading through even deeper mud as they made their way toward the barn.

"Hello!" Mommy called. "Is anyone in there?"

A chorus of bleating goats and a bawling calf answered her question. Then a man appeared in the doorway.

"You made it. Come on in and see what I got," he drawled

The old farmer wore old boots caked with mud, well-worn jeans, a striped button-up shirt, and suspenders. Naomi's eyes widened in surprise as she saw twenty or more goats looking back at her from inside the barn. Off to one side, a big barn cat sat on a bale of hay licking its paws. Soon the goats pushed around them. There were Nubian goats with long floppy ears, Boer goats with brown heads and white bodies, and LaMancha goats without outside ears.

"You can take your pick from this bunch," the farmer said, motioning toward some kid goats in the corner. "They're all young, maybe two weeks old. But I don't need um."

The children moved slowly over to the kids. Naomi smiled as a kid with big brown spots walked up and stood on her foot. She bent down and scratched the goat's back. Joseph was petting a cream colored kid.

"Are both of these kids LaMancha?" Naomi asked.

"Yep, they sure are. You can tell 'cause they don't have no ears. Ya like um?"

"Yes, I like this one; he is really friendly," Naomi said as she carefully picked up the kid.

"You can have him iffin you want him. I'd just sell him for meat once he gets big enough. Looks like you got one picked out, too," he said to Joseph. The boy smiled and nodded. "Now remember to feed these critters real careful. Don't give um too much food, or they'll get the runs and that's the end. Just feed um regular with good milk, and they'll do alright." Both children nodded solemnly.

Mommy helped Naomi and Joseph load the goats into the back of the van, and they drove home. When they got to their place, they tried to get the new babies settled in the little chicken house. It was much closer to the house and warmer then the barn, and for the time it would be the best place for the kids. When Lucky smelled the goats, she became very curious. She pressed her nose up against the wire of Bear's crate and wagged her stub tail. When Joseph opened the door of the crate and put the kids in the little pen, Lucky pushed in to see the new creatures. With typical baby innocence, the kids looked at the dog. Lucky sniffed them over carefully then began to lick their faces. Naomi's kid shook his head and walked away as if to say "I'm old enough to take care of myself, thank you!"

"Alright, Lucky, I don't think they want their faces washed before they even get their supper!" Naomi laughed. "Let's go fix up some formula for them! I bet they're hungry!"

Naomi walked toward the back door with Lucky at her heels. "Mommy, can we feed the babies yet?" she asked as she opened the door.

Mommy was just finishing washing some old baby bottles. "As soon as the formula is heated properly, we can go feed them." Mommy took the formula out of the microwave and carefully poured a drop on her wrist.

"What are you doing that for?" Naomi asked.

In reply Mommy poured a drop onto Naomi's wrist. "Can you feel the drop, Naomi?"

"No, I can't feel it at all, but I still don't understand why you did that!"

Mommy smiled. "It's to test the formula. If it's too hot, you would feel it burning your wrist, but if it is too cold, it would feel cool. We need the mixture to be warm. The wrist is the best place to test the temperature."

"May I test it again?" she asked. Mommy dropped some more on Naomi's wrist. "I think it is just right. Let's go feed those hungry babies!"

Naomi and Joseph tried getting the babies to drink from the bottle. Joseph held a bottle close to the mouth of one of the kids. The baby sniffed the strange thing then butted Joseph's hand hungrily. He smelled the milk but didn't know how to get it. Naomi and her kid were having the same challenges. The babies kept nuzzling the children's pant legs and poking them with their little noses. "Hey, Silly, that tickles!" Naomi laughed.

"I have an idea," Joseph said. He gently pinned the baby between his legs and cradled its chin in his hands. "There, now he can't get away."

He then put his thumb inside the kid's mouth. The baby started to suck! Then Joseph carefully replaced his thumb with the bottle. At first the goat blinked in surprise, and then he squeezed the nipple a little. Suddenly there was a transformation. The kid gave a happy little bleat, shook his little tail, and started to draw the warm liquid from the bottle. Soon Naomi's kid was draining its bottle, too.

"Look how hungry they are!" Naomi said. "I hope they won't get too hungry during the night! Do you think we should feed them before our morning chores?"

Joseph shook his head. "No, I think they will be just fine. After all, they were separated from their mothers early on, and I'm sure the farmer didn't feed them in the middle of the night!"

Naomi gave a little laugh. "No, I suppose he didn't."

Every day after that, the children carefully fed their

little babies. However, something was wrong. Instead of growing bigger and getting more active, the babies seemed to grow weaker. Their coats were rough, and they seemed to take less and less interest in food or their surroundings. One morning when the children went out to feed the babies their breakfast, they found one of the babies lying still and cold on the floor.

"What happened?" Naomi cried as she knelt by the little form. "We were so careful with our feedings and care of them." Her eyes filled with tears. "I can't believe he is dead!"

That morning the children had a hard time focusing on their lessons. Sadly they prepared the milk for the last kid at meal times. The baby seemed so lonely now. Soon they made another trip to see the farmer and get some more babies.

Unfortunately, the goats struggled to survive, even with the devoted care that Naomi and Joseph gave them. Over time they ended up with one baby that survived. It was Naomi's goat whom she named Barley. He was chocolate brown all over with white highlights. He was also a LaMancha.

Joseph got a goat from another family. He was full-grown and was also named Barley. Joseph's Barley was very big and rather ornery at times. He stood about three feet at the shoulders.

Mommy also got a goat, but her goat was a milk goat. She was creamy white with ears that stuck straight out from her head like airplane wings. They named her Daisy.

Life was exciting with their new four-legged additions to the farm. They quickly christened Joseph's goat "Big Barley," but he was ornery. Big Barley loved to try and grab poor Daisy by the ears as she ran by. The children made a small getaway pen for Daisy in the barn so she could have a safe place to run and hide from the bad-tempered Big Barley.

Chapter 6

Solving a Problem

~~~~~~~~~~~~~~~~~~

One day the children decided to take the goats for a walk along one of the many logging roads. Joseph fastened a strong rope to Big Barley's collar, and Naomi attached two lighter ropes to her "Little Barley" and Daisy. Lucky brought up the rear. But Big Barley didn't like having a dog behind him where he couldn't keep a good eye on it. He kept turning around and glaring at Lucky. Joseph had a hard time keeping Big Barley focused on the road in front of him. When Lucky turned her attention to the grass at the side of the road, Big Barley finally turned his attention back on the road and continued on with the children.

"Joseph, why don't we let the goats go? I'm sure they would follow us. It would be fun to see what they would do," Naomi suggested.

"Alright, why don't you let Little Barley and Daisy go first. I think they will stay close to us. If all goes well, then we can let Big Barley go too."

Naomi stopped and unclipped the leads of the two little goats, which looked up at her trustingly. Then turning as if nothing was different, Naomi began walking down the logging road. The two goats trotted after her, but all of a sudden they trotted on ahead of Naomi.

"Oh, no!" she exclaimed. "Do you think they will run away?"

Joseph smiled. "Look at them. Does it look like they are running away?"

Naomi looked again. Daisy and Little Barley had found a nice blackberry bush to nibble on and were working away at it as fast as they could. As soon as the children passed them, the goats trotted ahead until they found another juicy brush to nibble on.

"Why, they stick closer than most dogs!" Naomi said. "Well, all except for Lucky. She is always nearby ready to help!"

Naomi turned and smiled at Lucky who gave a little wiggle. She started forward toward Naomi, but then glanced at Big Barley. He was glaring at her again. Lucky looked longingly at Naomi. *Why does that big old goat have to bother Lucky?* she thought.

"I think I'll let Big Barley go," Joseph said. "He wants to eat some juicy leaves too!"

Big Barely ran ahead as soon as he was unleashed. He pushed his way between Daisy and Little Barley. Then he bit Daisy's ear and tried to bite Little Barley's as well. He finally settled down to munch on the fresh, new leaves of a salmonberry bush. The two smaller goats shook their heads and ran to the other side of the road to get away from the bully. Soon they were working on some other delicious foliage. Seeing her opening, Lucky bounded up to Naomi and wiggled all over. Naomi laughed and scratched Lucky behind the ears.

"Good girl, Lucky. That mean old goat has something else to keep his mind busy. He shouldn't pick on you so much."

For the rest of the walk, Lucky stayed as close as she could to Naomi. Whenever Big Barley went running past to find something else to eat, Lucky eyed him carefully from Naomi's side.

The children took the goats out more and more as the summer went on. When they couldn't take them on a walk, they let them out into the horse pasture to graze on the ever-present blackberry bushes. However, it became more and more difficult to bring them back in from the field each evening. The goats quickly learned that when the children appeared and called them it was time to go in. Instead of coming to the children, they would run to the far side of the field and eat as quickly as possible until they were caught. Once Big Barley was caught, the other two would usually follow.

One day when it was Naomi's turn to put the goats away, they were especially feisty. When they saw her and Lucky quietly approaching, they whirled around, stuck their tails in the air, and bounced away. "Sometimes I wonder if they think they are deer," Naomi commented to Lucky.

She calmly walked to the far end of the field and tried to corner Big Barley. However, the large goat did not want to go back into his boring pen. For several minutes he and the girl played ring-around-the-blackberry bush. The goat would eat as fast as he could until Naomi was almost within reach of his collar, then he would dash to the other side of the bush. Naomi sighed. It was impossible to walk through the blackberry bush because the thorns hurt her bare feet. Carefully she walked around the big bush until she was close to him again. This time Big Barley reared up on his hind legs, pinned his ears back, and acted as if he was going to butt Naomi with his big head. On his hind legs, he was taller than Naomi, so she quickly took a step back.

"Now come on Big Barley," she said in a firm voice. "Quit being such a bully! I'm not afraid of you!"

The goat ran off to another tempting bush. The girl doggedly followed. This time she was able to get close enough to scratch his back. That was one of his weaknesses. At once he seemed to forget about the tempting leaves just begging to be eaten. He slowly lifted his head, licked his lips, and closed his eyes. Naomi carefully reached forward and wrapped her fingers around his collar. The goat didn't seem to notice. The girl continued to scratch him for a few more moments. Once she had a firm grip on his collar, she said, "Alright, big guy, it's time to go to the barn." When the goat felt the pull on his collar, he braced his feet.

"Up to your old tricks again, huh, buddy?" Naomi stepped to the left, pulling the goat off center, then she walked to the right. Big Barley took a few steps. Next she pulled back on the collar as if trying to stop the goat from walking at all. Big Barley lunged ahead, running as fast as he could for the barn.

"You crazy old goat! Why don't you just walk nicely to

the barn?" Naomi panted as she jogged along. Suddenly she had an idea. Pulling as hard as she could on his collar, she slowed him down enough to vault onto his back as if he was a horse. Big Barley screeched to a halt and turned and looked at Naomi.

She laughed. "What's the matter, old goat? Don't you mind if I catch a ride?"

Naomi pulled on his collar again, and Big Barley put his head down and ran as fast as he could for the barn. She was laughing so hard she could hardly stay on. Her feet ran along with his, so as not to put her full weight on him, which might injure his back. Daisy and Little Barley were already in the pen watching the rodeo with wide eyes. They gave little snorts of alarm. Suddenly Big Barley changed his course and charged toward a small tree.

"Oh no! Big Barley, you wouldn't dare!" Naomi gasped, but Big Barley did dare. Ducking his head, he squeezed under the lowest branches.

"Alright! Alright, I give up!" Naomi said as she toppled in a heap under the tree. Being released of his burden, he bounded for the safety of the barn. Naomi was laughing so hard she could hardly stand up. She rocked back and forth on the ground holding her sides.

"That crazy old goat! I'll have to do that again!" When she opened her eyes, Lucky was standing over her with a concerned look on her face. "Lucky, did you see me ride Big Barley almost all the way to the barn! It was so fun!"

Lucky's face was covered in dirt, and her nose was brown.

"Have you been after a mole again? Did you get it? Let me see what you were doing." Naomi said as she fastened the gate. Lucky led her proudly to the molehill that she had been working on.

"Wow, Lucky! Did you almost get him?" Naomi said. "Hey, what about this one over here!" She pointed to a large fresh molehill. Lucky tensed as she stared at the molehill. Then slowly she walked toward it. She leaned forward, sniffed it carefully, and then rocked back on her haunches. Naomi began to count slowly, "One... Twooooooooo... THREE! Dig, Lucky! DIG!"

The dog jumped forward like a fox and started digging furiously. When she found the tunnel, she jammed her nose down as far as it would go and sniffed and snorted. After a few moments, she backed out of the hole, her whole head covered in dirt. She glanced at Naomi, but she had a funny look on her face.

"What's wrong, Lucky?" Naomi asked.

Wrinkling up her face, Lucky let out a big sneeze.

"Did you get dirt up your nose? I would too if I stuck my nose in the dirt and sniffed around!" Naomi laughed. "You are a good girl. I bet you chased that old mole clean out of the country!"

That evening at supper, Naomi retold the story of riding Big Barley. Daddy's eyes twinkled. Then he said. "Why don't you train the goats to come when you call? It sounds to me like that would be much easier in the long run."

Naomi put down her fork. "How in the world could I train Big Barley to do anything? He is so stubborn!"

Daddy smiled. "I think you can figure it out. Just give it some thought."

After supper, Naomi and Lucky practiced their 4-H exercises. Practicing the recall was the most fun. Naomi would tell Lucky to sit, and then she would walk to the other end of the yard. When the girl stopped and turned to face the dog, Lucky would be leaning forward in anticipation. Sometimes Lucky would begin to come before Naomi called her. Jeanne had told her not to scold Lucky for this, but she was to take the dog back and have her sit again. Then she should walk away, turn, wait for a few seconds, and then call her. Lucky loved this exercise. When Naomi did call Lucky, the dog bolted as fast as she could, sliding to a stop in front of Naomi.

"OK, Lucky! Good girl! Go get the ball!" Naomi threw it with all her might. It was more of a game than anything.

After they had finished practicing, Naomi and Lucky went to do the chores. As they fed the goats, Daddy's words came back to her about training the goats. Naomi scratched Big Barley's back.

"How in the world could I teach you to do anything? You always try and do the exact opposite of what I ask! When I want you to walk forward, you stop. When I want you to stop, you run as fast as you can. When we want you to stay away from the little goat's food, that is all you want! You step on people's feet, you chase Lucky, and you bite poor Daisy's ears! What in the world can we do with you?" Big Barley grabbed a mouthful of hay and chewed it thoughtfully.

"I thought Tillie was stubborn, but she was trainable with a ball! You don't even like toys!" Big Barley swallowed the hay and sniffed Naomi's hands.

"Would you work for food, Barley?" Naomi poured a little grain into a feeding pan. When Big Barley heard the oats falling into the pan, he stopped eating and pushed his nose as close to the pan as possible. The other goats crowded around, too.

"Well, what do you know! It just might be possible to teach you something after all!" Giving the goats a little taste of the much-wanted grain, Naomi then left the pen and headed for the house. After telling Joseph and Mommy about her idea, Naomi found a bell.

"I think I will teach them to come to this! They would be able to hear this easier than my voice at a long distance."

Naomi, Joseph, and Lucky quickly walked back out to the goats. The goats had left their barn and were playing in their grassy pen. The children quickly put a little grain in a pan and went outside. Joseph shook the pan so the goats could hear the grain, and when they began running towards them, Naomi rang the bell. In the following days, each time they fed them grain they rang the bell. Soon, the goats were racing as fast as they could as soon as they heard the bell.

Chapter 7

The Hidden Meadow

~~~~~~~~~~~~~~~~~~~~~~

The day was cold and rainy. A weak light filtered into the old barn where a wide-eyed horse stood in a stall. She lifted her head in alarm as the rain pounded with renewed strength on the metal roof. Taking a mouthful of hay, the horse turned to face the doorway that led into the pasture. She couldn't decide if it would be better to go out in the pasture and get wet or to stay inside with the constant noise.

Grabbing another mouthful of hay, she chose to take the rain over the noise. Carefully stepping out to avoid as much mud as possible, the nineteen-year-old Arabian mare entered her small pasture. She had only been in this new place for two days and was still adjusting to her surroundings. Restlessly, she paced the fence line. She tossed her head as if to say, "Where is that girl and dog? I'm getting hungry for the delicious grain she had!"

At last she heard the back door shut. The horse stopped pacing and lifted her head toward the sound. Her delicate ears flicked forward. When the girl and dog came into sight, she tossed her head again and nickered. *At last! Grain time!* Eagerly she entered the barn. When the girl and dog arrived, she impatiently bobbed her head up and down. It seemed to take forever for the girl to pour the grain into a bucket and give it to her.

"There you go, Jayla. Here's your supper. Has it been a long day for you, old horse?" Naomi tossed hay into the manger. Carefully Naomi ran her fingers through the horse's black mane. It was very long and reached almost to the point of the mare's shoulder.

"I don't understand how your hair always gets tangled, girl! You seem to enjoy getting it all messed up so that I have to untangle it every evening." Naomi laughed as she glanced at Lucky. "I guess I'm starting to sound like a mother, aren't I, doggie."

Lucky gave a little wiggle and looked up at Naomi with a grin. For several minutes Naomi quietly worked the knots out of the horse's mane. Then she braided it into even braids.

"Lucky, would you get me that curry comb over there?" Naomi asked. Lucky jumped off the hay bales where she had been inspecting the barn cat and looked up at Naomi.

"Over there, Lucky. Go get it!" The dog ran over and picked up the curry comb.

"Come, Lucky." Lucky trotted over to the girl.

"Give it. OK, Lucky, good girl! Go play with the kitty again!" Turning back to the horse, she slowly worked over the horse's neck, sides, and rump. Going to the other side, she started the process over again. Jayla finished her grain, turned her head, and gave Naomi a friendly shove.

"Hey, there! Who are you trying to push around?" Naomi laughed. "I'm almost done, and then you can go out in the rain again if you want. Why don't you eat your hay?" The horse sighed and turned back to the manger. As she began to eat, she idly watched Lucky stare at the cat.

The cat sat on the highest hay bale and glared back at the dog. Her tail swished back and forth—her ears were pressed against her head. She eyed the dog coldly. Lucky slowly climbed up on the hay bale just below the cat. There, Lucky sat for a few minutes as if trying to decide her next move. The cat let out a low growl.

"Lucky, it looks to me like the cat isn't enjoying your company. I would be careful if I was you!"

Lucky reared up on her hind legs and thrust her nose toward the angry cat. Quick as a flash, the mad feline swatted the dog on her nose. Lucky yelped in surprise and toppled off the hay. "Poor puppy, did you just learn that sometime kitties aren't as friendly as you would like them to be?" The dog glanced back at the cat. The kitty stood and calmly stretched and then lay down again.

"Lucky, it is time for us to go in for supper. Come on; let's see who can get to the house first!" The two dashed through the rain, Lucky easily winning the short race.

"It's not fair! You have two more legs than I do, so naturally you can run twice as fast!" Naomi laughed.

After a few weeks, the rain finally relented to the sun, and the trees began to shake out their leaves to dry. When the sun shown, Naomi had an even harder time concentrating on her schoolwork. All she could think of was going outside to play with Lucky or ride Jayla. Joseph always seemed to be able to concentrate and get all his schoolwork done shortly after noon. When he went outside, it was even harder for Naomi to think about math or spelling.

One day after taking a longer time than normal to finish her work, Naomi raced out of the house as soon as she completed the last math problem.

"Lucky, come! Let's go ride the horse!" Naomi called. Grabbing her helmet and a bridle, she ran into the field. Jayla was standing near the far fence looking intently into the other field.

"Did Becky already come and ride Shadow somewhere? Did we miss them?" Naomi said to Lucky as she climbed up on the fence and looked around. "Yep, I think they must be gone. I see Foxy running around. It looks like she is worried and wondering where Shadow has gone."

Naomi climbed down from the fence and began putting the bridle on Jayla. "We had better hurry. You know how fast Shadow can be. The only problem is that I'm not sure which way they went."

Naomi led the horse to a rock. When she stood on the rock, she was able to grab a handful of mane and swing onto Jayla's back. As soon as she was halfway on, the horse began to trot toward the gate.

"Jayla, can't you wait until I am sitting on you before you take off? Oh well, I'm on now, let's get going!" When they reached the house, Naomi pulled the horse to a stop next to the front room window. From inside, Mommy saw them and came to the window and opened it.

"I'm going to go ride with Becky. She has already taken off. Is that alright?" Naomi asked.

"Yes, that is fine. Don't be gone too long," Mommy replied.

Naomi loosened the reins, and Jayla started out at a brisk trot. "I don't know how we will catch up with her, but let's give it a try. I think we'll look in the woods across the river first."

Once they crossed the bridge, she slowed the horse down again. "Lucky, I need your help." The dog looked up at her, sensing the urgency in her voice. "Go find Becky!" Naomi excitedly instructed.

Lucky looked a little confused. She knew what "go find" meant, but who was Becky? She sniffed the air and then sniffed the ground. Suddenly she took off running with her nose to the ground. Lucky turned onto a trail that the girls often rode on. Naomi leaned over her trotting horse and studied the ground. *Yes, there are fresh horse tracks! Becky did go this way. Lucky understands!*

"Good girl, Lucky!" Naomi called. "Go find Becky!"

She reached for a better hold on Jayla's mane. The horse had no trouble keeping up with the running dog. But Lucky suddenly swerved off the trail. Naomi pulled the horse to a stop.

"Did Becky go off the trail, Lucky?" she asked. "I'm not sure if Jayla can go through the woods. The ground is covered with thick brush and logs." Naomi looked down the trail. She didn't see any hoof prints, but she figured Lucky knew what she was doing.

"Well, Lucky, you are the one that can smell her. I'm going to trust you."

Naomi turned Jayla off the trail. It was rough going, but Jayla handled the new terrain like a pro. Naomi often had to call to Lucky to slow down and wait for them since it was much easier for her to move through the woods than the horse. Soon, the trees became very thick, and the logs on the ground more numerous. As they pushed through some more brush they came upon a big surprise.

"Whoa, Jayla! Did you ever see anything like it?"

Before them lay the most beautiful clearing. It had a little pond on one side, and there was grass growing instead of brush. A few logs lay at the border of the clearing. Two ducks took to wing and flew over her head. Lucky didn't seem to notice the beauty around her. She ran down into the meadow, up the other side, and into the trees.

"Lucky! Wait!" Naomi called. Jayla slowly walked into the meadow. She was tired. Naomi slid off her back and examined the horse's legs. Carefully she ran her hand down each leg.

"It looks like you got a little scratched up, didn't you, girl?" Naomi said. "We had better not go on. There's no telling how brushy it will be over there. It would be easier on you to go back on the trail we already made."

Naomi straightened up again. "Lucky, come!"

Soon the brown-and-white dog appeared through the trees. "Lucky, you are such a good girl, but I don't think we should continue to track Becky. Jayla's legs are scratched up, and we don't know what it will be like farther on. Do you understand? Let's just rest here for a little while, then we'll go back home. Maybe Becky will be there by then." The girl sat down on a nearby log, and Lucky leaned against her.

After a few moments rest, Naomi climbed back on Jayla, and they headed for home on the trail they had cut through the trees. When they got to the field, they were surprised to find Becky. As soon as she saw them, she hurried over.

"You'll never guess what I found! I was in the woods, and I found the prettiest little clearing! I'll have to show it to you some time!"

Naomi smiled. "Well, I have something to tell you, too. I told Lucky to track you, and she led me to that clearing! It *is* beautiful! We'll have to visit it together sometime! We would have kept on following you, but Jayla's legs were getting scratched up, so we decided to turn around."

"Wow, Lucky actually tracked me all that way? That is amazing! She sure is a good dog!" Becky said.

That evening Naomi and Lucky sprawled out on the bedroom floor together. Lucky happily snoozed while Naomi studied her 4-H questions. One hand held the paper while the other stroked Lucky's soft fur. She was so proud of her dog. *Thank you, Jesus, for giving me Lucky. She has been a very big blessing in my life. I can't imagine life without her now.*

Chapter 8

Feeding the Animals

~~~~~~~~~~~~~~~~~~

Naomi glanced at her watch. It was time to feed the animals and bed them down for the night. She could hear Joseph and Mommy talking in the front room.

"Lucky! Wake up! We're going to sneak out and feed all the animals before Joseph finds out!" Naomi giggled.

Joseph and Naomi made an endless game of trying to feed all the animals before the other knew what was going on. There were two different pens of goats to feed and put in the barn; Daisy to milk; rabbits and Jayla to feed; as well as a flock of free-ranging ducks and chickens to find and pen up for the night. It usually was impossible to finish everything before the other person got suspicious, but it was always fun to try. Naomi carefully put her 4-H questions away, put on a light jacket, and slowly opened her window. The window was old and always complained whenever it was opened or shut.

"I'm sure Joseph is listening for me to go out the back door, Lucky. But he won't know we left if we just jump out the window!" Lucky put her paws on the windowsill and looked out.

"You can make it, girl! It isn't very far to the ground! Just follow me!"

Naomi jumped. When she turned around and looked back at the window, Lucky was still peering over the windowsill. "Come on. You can do it!" Naomi encouraged. "Let's go feed the animals!"

When Lucky heard that, her head disappeared for a moment. Then she burst through the open window.

"Good girl! That's the way! It is kind of hard to get up the courage the first time, isn't it?"

In no time, they were in the barn. They fed the goats and Jayla as quickly as possible, and then they whistled for the ducks. The majority of the ducks were a tall, dark, skinny breed called Indian runners. And just like their name implies, they ran everywhere, even when they were hunting for slugs! It was as if they were afraid the slugs would out run them.

One of her favorite runners was a drake named Ferdinand. When someone was within sight of his flock of girls, he would run up to them and gently pull on their pant leg. This was his way of showing that he was a big, mean duck.

Behind them came a big, fat, blue-grey duck the children called the Blue Goose. She was a meat duck that always huffed and puffed as she tried to keep up with the hyperactive runners.

Following close behind the Blue Goose were two brown ducks. They were sisters; one was called "The Mean Duck" because she always seemed to be in a bad mood. The other was named Scruffy. Her feathers were often messed up, and she never seemed to care. Naomi sat down next to the duck pen. The ducks swarmed around her, poking their bills into her coat and pant pockets. They were hunting for the grain that was sure to be there. Naomi looked up and whistled again. One duck was still missing.

Quack! Quack! Quack!

"Come, Gimpy! Supper time!" Naomi called.

A family who lived in town had given the children Gimpy. The family had rescued the duck from a dog, but since they had nowhere to keep her, they gave her to Joseph and Naomi. One of her legs was badly mangled. Naomi had tried to bandage it, but Gimpy's leg had never healed properly. In the end, she couldn't walk like a normal duck. She had to hop on her good foot and use her bad one as a crutch. For that reason, the other ducks always left her behind. Naomi admired Gimpy for her courage. She didn't seem to worry about her handicap. She happily went about her duck business at a more comfortable pace. Naomi stood up and herded the main flock into their house. When she turned around, Gimpy was sitting at her feet.

"Good girl, Gimpy. Did you have a good day?" Naomi asked as she gave Gimpy a handful of grain. After finishing her grain and getting a sip of water, she was ready for bed. Naomi carefully opened the door of the duck pen and pushed the other ducks back while Gimpy made her way inside.

With that chore done, she moved on to the next one. "Come on, Lucky. Let's go take care of the Barleys, rabbits, and chickens. Then we can milk Daisy!"

Just then Naomi heard the back door slam, and Joseph came running out. "Naomiiiiii! Are you trying to get all the chores done without me knowing about it?" Joseph yelled.

Naomi ran as fast as she could for the goat pen, but Joseph was faster.

"OK, OK, I give up!" Naomi laughed. "Lucky and I almost had everything done! All that's left to do is milk

Daisy, feed the Barleys and the rabbits, and put the chickens to bed."

Joseph turned to her. "I'm going to do those things. You've already done more then you were supposed to do!"

Chapter 9

Bear and the Electric Fence

~~~~~~~~~~~~~~~~

Jayla sighed as Naomi led her up to the hitching post. She had hoped to spend a few more hours basking in the sunshine. "It's OK, Jayla," Naomi consoled, "you can enjoy the sunshine just as much at the hitching post as in the field."

After tying the horse to the hitching post, Naomi ran into the barn to get some brushes. "Lucky, come help me take these brushes outside," Naomi called when she realized she couldn't carry everything.

Lucky willingly came to her side. "Here, you take the curry comb—that's your favorite one to carry—and I'll take the rest."

Lucky picked up the curry comb and pranced out the door of the barn. Naomi scooped up the rest of the grooming supplies and followed her out of the barn. Naomi began to curry Jayla from her neck and along her sides and rump. After she had completed one side with the curry, she brushed the same area again with a soft bristled brush. This brush took all the loose dirt and hair off that the curry comb had loosened. Then Naomi repeated the same procedure again on the other side of the horse. She then carefully brushed Jayla's face and rubbed a little fly spray around her eyes. Next Naomi picked up a comb and began to untangle Jayla's long mane.

"I don't see how you can get your mane so dirty and tangled, old horse," Naomi stated to her animal friend. Jayla just closed her eyes and swished her tail.

"Naomi, are you getting ready to go on a trail ride?" Joseph asked as he walked toward her. Bear walked beside Joseph on a lease. He was too independent to be allowed to run free. He'd rather do his own thing than to do as he was told.

"I was planning on going for a ride, but I don't have too if you want to do something else," Naomi replied.

"I was thinking of walking down to the Deep Hole, but if you are busy, I can go by myself," Joseph said.

"That sounds like fun! We haven't been down there for a while. We might be able to find some good salmonberries along the trail," Naomi said. "Let me finish grooming Jayla, and then I'll be ready to go."

Joseph smiled. "Here, let me help you finish up." He quickly tied Bear up to a large piece of wood and ducked under the electric fence. "I'll pick out her feet while you finish her mane. Alright?"

Naomi nodded. "Sounds good to me." The siblings worked in silence for a few minutes. "When do you think Daddy will be able to finish the big pasture fence?" Naomi asked. "Jayla has been in this little electric fence for quite a while."

Joseph slowly straightened up after picking out one of Jayla's feet. "I'm not sure. His only free time to really get a lot done on the fence is on Sunday, and he has a lot of other things to do around here too. Besides, we don't have all the fencing we need yet. Once we get that and Daddy shows me what to do, I'm sure I can work on it after I'm done with my schoolwork. That is, if you will help me. It's for your horse after all!" Joseph teased.

"Of course I'll help. You know I'll do what I can," Naomi said. "Well, I think we are about done for now. I'll go and put these brushes away, and then I'll be ready to go to the Deep Hole with you."

Naomi unbuckled Jayla's halter and then picked up the brushes. "Lucky, do you want to go to the Deep Hole?" Naomi asked. Lucky dropped the bone she had been chewing on and ran over to her, wiggling all over.

"OK, as soon as I put away these brushes, we can go for a walk."

Realizing she was untied, Jayla tossed her head and hurried toward the pasture. Lucky ran after Jayla and jumped at her head to stop her from getting away. "It's OK, Lucky. We'll go for a ride after we get back from our walk. Let Jayla go," Naomi called.

Lucky came back to Naomi and looked up apologetically, "Don't worry, doggie. You were trying to help. You didn't understand our change in plans. You're a good girl!"

Naomi hurried into the barn and put the brushes away. Just as she emerged again, Bear let out a yelp of surprise.

"Oh no! Bear's tail just touched the electric fence!" Joseph cried. Bear took off for home as fast as he could go. The big block of wood he was tied too bounced along behind him. Bear looked over his shoulder and saw the menacing block jumping after him. A look of panic came over his face, and he ran even faster for the house. Joseph and Naomi called for him to stop, but he seemed to run faster as he desperately tried to get away from the terrible piece of wood that had bit him in the tail and was now chasing him home! Lucky ran after Bear and got in front of him in an attempt to slow him down, but Bear just dodged Lucky and ran faster.

"Poor dog!" Naomi gasped. "We'd better catch him before he hurts himself."

Both children hurried after the frightened dog. After a few minutes they caught him and untied him from his antagonist. He was panting hard.

"Everything is alright, Bear," Joseph reassured him. "It was my fault to tie you that close to the fence. Poor, Bear."

Bear wagged his tail a little and licked Joseph's hand. He seemed to forgive and forget easily.

Joseph looked at Naomi. "It *was* funny watching him run for the house like that with the wood bouncing behind him," Joseph chuckled. "I wouldn't want him to go through that again, but it was funny!"

Naomi laughed. "It reminded me of the time I put those big white buckets on Jayla, so she could haul sand for me. She bolted and ran right through the electric fence and jumped part of the other fence. Do you remember?"

"Yes, I do," replied Joseph. "Jayla isn't a pack horse, and those scary white buckets bouncing on her back was just too much for her to take! And then after we caught her, we had to fix both fences."

Naomi doubled over in laughter. "And just as we had finished repairing the electric fence, you were saying that you had not been shocked yet, remember?"

Joseph looked at Naomi with a wry smile. "I'd just as soon not talk about it."

"But it was sooo funny!" Naomi sputtered. "Just as

you said that, you went under the fence and a piece of extra wire you were carrying touched the hot wire. You and all the tools you were carrying went flying!" Naomi bent over again in laughter.

"I suppose it was kind of funny being the spectator. It sure was a surprise," Joseph grinned. "I guess we should get going on that walk."

And with that, the children and dogs headed down the road.

Chapter 10

The Pack Trip

~~~~~~~~~~~~~~~~~

"Let's see. Do we have everything?" Naomi said as she carefully packed her backpack. "I still need to get my flashlight and Bible. There they are," Naomi said as she reached for the items on top of her dresser. "Now, all we have to do is load up the Barleys and pack the car."

Naomi headed toward the kitchen. "Come on, Lucky! Let's go check Little Barley's pack—he is carrying your food!" The girl and the dog hurried onto the back porch and grabbed Little Barley's pack off the washing machine. Naomi carefully checked the pockets.

"Here is your food, Lucky, and here is some extra rope. We should put some grain in the other side to even it out for him." Naomi and Lucky ran out to the barn and got a small bag of grain. "This should do it!"

By the time they got back to the house, Joseph had already led Big Barley up to the back porch to test the weight and balance of his goat's pack. Big Barley had a genuine goat pack. It looked just like a miniature mule pack. It had wooden cross beams and straps that looped around the front of the goat and another behind. This would keep the pack from sliding too far forward or too far back when he went up or down hills. The pack also had a cinch that went under him and fit snuggly just behind the front legs. Uncle David and his children, Jonathan and Joanna, and their dog, Bobby, came into the yard with their backpacks.

Mommy came out of the house. "Are you sure you have everything? Do you have the rope to tie up the goats at night?"

"Yes, I have it in here," Joseph answered, patting his backpack.

Daddy pulled the truck up to the front of the house. After loading the packs, they coaxed the goats into the back. Joseph, Sarah, Naomi, and Lucky climbed into the cab of the truck. Uncle David and his children followed in their car. When they got to the trailhead, Daddy helped them unload the goats and gear.

"I'll come pick you up tomorrow afternoon. I hope you have a good time!" Daddy said as he got back into the truck and drove away. The Barleys were already munching on some nearby salmonberry bushes.

"Hey, goats! We aren't going on a picnic. This is a hike, and everyone has to carry their own pack! Even you, guys!" Naomi said as she pulled her goat away from his snack.

"You can nibble as we go, but first I have to put your pack on you." Little Barley stood still as Naomi carefully secured his pack. It didn't weigh very much, so it wasn't a big deal to him. Big Barley, on the other hand, had much more weight to carry. He had been delegated to carry the supply of drinking water because he was a big, strong goat.

Lucky ran around from person to person. She was just happy to be allowed to come along. Most of the time when Naomi started stuffing things in a bag, Lucky knew she was leaving her. But this time she was going too!

Soon the expedition headed down the trail. Sarah led the way with Jonathan, Joanna, and Bobby following. Uncle David came next in line with Lucky, Naomi, and Little Barley. Behind them came Joseph with Big Barley. After a few minutes the children let the Barleys loose. The little goat ran ahead to snatch a few more leaves. After everyone caught up, he would run ahead again.

The trail soon became steeper as it wound its way up the side of a mountain. The goal was to reach the top by nightfall, set up camp, and then hike around the next day before meeting Daddy again at the trailhead. Big Barley began to fall further and further behind. He was beginning to breathe hard because of his heavy pack. Soon, he was walking slowly.

"Uncle David!" Joseph called. "We need to stop for a minute. Big Barley is getting too far behind us."

Everyone was happy to take a little break. The large goat slowly continued to climb. When he was about fifty feet from the rest of the group, he stopped and looked at everyone. With a determined look in his eye, he turned around and started trotting down the mountain trail.

"Oh no!" everyone yelled. "Big Barley, come back! We need all that water you are carrying!"

Joseph dropped his pack and charged after his goat.

"We might as well sit down and wait for them to come back. There is no use in all of us chasing him down the trail!" Uncle David laughed

About thirty minutes later, Joseph came trudging up the trail leading Big Barley.

"How far did he go?" Sarah asked.

"Almost all the way to the parking lot!" Joseph replied. "I think I will leave him on the lead for the rest of the hike!

I don't want to put up with anymore of his shenanigans!"

By that evening the group had reached a camping spot near the top of the ridge. After securing the goats and setting up the tents, the tired group ate a cold supper of trail mix and granola bars.

Naomi did not sleep well that night. A cold wind blew up the mountain and seemed to continue right through the tent walls. If that weren't bad enough, Lucky wouldn't settle down. Every few minutes she would get up and growl at the forest noises.

The goats didn't sleep either. At first they contented themselves with chewing their cud. But after that job was finished, they stomped around as far as the rope would let them. Several times during the night Joseph and Naomi got up to check on them. Then around two o'clock in the morning as Naomi went to check on the noisy goats, Lucky charged up the hill, barking furiously. In a few minutes, she returned, panting and out of breath.

"What were you chasing, girl?" Naomi asked. Lucky growled again and looked up the hill.

"Is everything alright?" Uncle David asked.

"Whatever it was, Lucky chased it away!"

The rest of the night passed quietly. The goats finally settled down and didn't seem to make so much noise. Even though it was a rough night sleep, morning came and the group spent a fun day hiking and exploring the top of the ridge.

Before long it was time to pack everything up and head back to the trailhead where they were to meet Daddy. As they reached the truck, Naomi excitedly told her dad about the events of the last two days.

Chapter 11

The Steadfast Duck

~~~~~~~~~~~~~~~~~~~~

"Have you seen Scruffy lately?" Joseph asked as he milked Daisy one evening. The milk made a cheery zinging sound as it hit the bottom of the milk pail. The sound soon became muffled as the level of milk rose and the sweet smell of warm milk filled the barn. Lucky sniffed around at the base of the stanchion for dropped grain and other goodies.

"No, I haven't seen her today. I wonder if she has gone broody on us again. Lucky and I will go see if we can find her."

Daisy finished her grain and stood calmly on the wooden stanchion as Joseph finished the milking.

"Lucky, come!" Naomi called. The dog stopped her investigation and trotted over to the girl. "Scruffy is missing, and we are going to look for her!" she told her companion.

Naomi and Lucky carefully searched the bushes and tall grass around the goat barn. No luck. "Let's go look by the alder tree by the Barleys' pen." Naomi said. "There are some good places for a duck to hide a nest there. Lucky, go find Scruffy!"

At Naomi's command, Lucky began to plow through the tall grass. She swung her head back and forth, searching for the duck's scent in the air. Naomi smiled. She loved watching her dog hunt for something. She could tell that Lucky loved doing jobs like this.

The eager dog paused for a moment. She stared intently into a large clump of grass. Her stub tail wiggled, and she looked back at Naomi with a happy doggy grin.

"Did you find that old duck, Lucky?" Naomi asked as she waded into the tall grass. Lucky thrust her head into the grass, and the girl heard angry quacking.

"Good girl! I knew you could do it!"

Naomi peered into the clump of grass where the sound came from. Sure enough, there was Scruffy. Her feathers were all ruffled, and she slowly rocked back and forth on her collection of eggs.

Then she spread her wings over her eggs and stretched out her neck, quacking in her meanest voice. "You sure look like an ornery old duck, but I know you aren't that mean," Naomi laughed.

Naomi reached her hand toward the duck. As soon as she touched the duck's feathers, Scruffy changed her tune. Instead of quacking angrily, she quietly talked to Naomi in friendly little squeaks. Her feathers went down, and she let Naomi see her eggs.

"Well, Scruffy, you got yourself a fine bunch of eggs. I hope you will stay on the nest long enough this time to hatch them!"

Naomi slowly backed away from the duck's nest. "Lucky, we are going to have to keep an eye on her while she is broody. We don't want anything to hurt or bother her. Maybe this time she will stay on the nest longer than just a few hours or days! I guess the mothering instinct in her isn't as strong as in most ducks."

Naomi walked back to the barnyard. When she reached

the door to the Barleys' barn, she grabbed a handful of grain and whistled for the ducks and chickens. In a few seconds, three runners came running, slapping their webbed feet on the dry ground. Naomi tossed the grain up in the air and watched it fall to the earth.

The chickens scurried in from another direction. There were five chickens, all bantams. There was the rooster named Henry the First and his hen named Penny. Then there were three young chickens: one brown hen, a black rooster, and one small white rooster. The white one was Naomi's favorite. She had named him Billy the Great, and she often carried him everywhere.

Billy probably told feather-raising stories to the other chickens. Naomi would often put him in her coat pocket and climb high into a tree. Once perched on a limb, she would take him out so he could get a "bird's-eye view" of their home. Other times, she would take him for a ride on Jayla. Naomi learned that Billy enjoyed the ride as long as she kept the horse at a walk. It was a little better on the bike. Billy would hang onto the handlebars, squat low, and spread his wings. If Naomi didn't make any sharp turns, Billy was able to stay on for the whole ride.

One day Naomi discovered that her chicken was even able to float on his back! It was a warm day, and Naomi thought that poor Billy was too warm and would like to be cooled off by a nice bath. She proceeded to get a bucket of water. Billy held very still as she carefully lowered him into the water. After getting him good and wet, she held Billy on his back in the palm of her hand. Being such a cooperative chicken, he again held perfectly still.

I wonder if he could float on his back, she thought. Slowly she lowered the chicken once more into the water. When Billy felt the water on his back, he spread his wings. When Naomi took her hand away, there floated Billy as calm as could be.

"Billy! You are a very talented rooster!" Naomi cried. "You might even become famous with a talent like that! Just think! A rooster that can float on its back!"

Billy looked at her with his head cocked at a funny angle, his feet pointing straight up, and his long tail lying in the water like a rudder.

Naomi's thoughts were jerked back to the present. The flock of ducks and chickens swarmed at her feet, each trying to eat as much of the grain as possible. Ferdinand the male duck pushed his way past Penny the hen to get a nice big kernel of corn. Penny squawked in protest. All of a sudden there was a flurry of feathers. The ducks and young chickens began flapping their wings and running as fast they could in every direction.

"Henry! What do you think you are doing chasing all the ducks and other chickens away? They didn't mean any harm. Sure, they might push you and your wife around a little, but that's OK, isn't it?"

Henry didn't think so. He puffed up his feathers and gave a defiant crow. One of the runners approached for another try. Henry crouched down, spread his wings, and glared at the duck. However, ducks have very short memories, and this one didn't even seem to notice the tiny rooster ready to spring on her at any moment.

"Watch out, ducky! That mean, old rooster is trying to impress his girl! You'd better stay away!" Naomi cautioned.

But the duck kept coming. She had her eyes on all that wonderful grain just laying there on the ground. When she was about a foot away from the rooster, Henry launched himself through the air, his little spurs trying to make contact with the surprised duck. There was a flurry of feathers and once again the defeated duck was on the run. Henry crowed again as if to say, "Now, tell me who the chickens are around here!"

Seeing that the ducks had given up for the moment, he turned back to Penny and the grain. But lo and behold, there was Gimpy gobbling the grain as fast as she could. She had quietly approached while he was busy chasing the other ducks. Henry crouched in front of Gimpy. The duck stopped eating and stared back at the rooster. She wasn't going to run from that tiny little feather puff. For a moment everyone was still. Then, as before, Henry leaped through the air, but Gimpy was ready. Gimpy lowered her head and Henry sailed over, landing on the duck's back. Quick as a wink, Gimpy reached around and grabbed a beak full of that beautiful tail. *Squawk!* yelled Henry.

But Gimpy wasn't done yet. She stood up on her one good leg and pivoted around in a circle while Henry tried in vain to get away. After a few moments, Gimpy relented and let go of the humiliated rooster. From then on, Henry had a healthy respect for that courageous duck with the crippled leg.

Chapter 12

Summer Fun

~~~~~~~~~~~~~~~~~~~~~~~~

"I wonnnder, does anybody happen to want to gooooooo outside with me?"

Bear was on his feet in a moment. Bear danced around and whined, then ran to the front door. Lucky pushed her nose under Naomi's arm.

The girl laughed. "Are you both sure you really want to go outside?" she asked again. Bear was back beside the couch in a flash. He fixed his big brown eyes on her and gave a big bark, then charged back to the front door. Lucky stood up, shook, then also ran to the front door.

"OK, I guess both of you want to. Let's hook you up to in the harnesses first. Where did I leave those, anyway?" Naomi mumbled to herself.

After finding the harnesses, she quickly slipped them on the eager dogs. The homemade harnesses had a wide soft strap that went across each dog's chest and attached behind the dog's front legs. It was a very simple harness, but it seemed to do the job quite nicely. After slipping the harnesses over the dog's heads and buckling them, Naomi attached the two dogs together by a short lead, and then hooked another longer lead to the short one. Lucky and Bear waited at the door. They could hardly wait to get outside and run.

"Just a minute you two! I have to put on my roller-blades!" Naomi said.

"Naomi, don't be gone too long. It is almost time for lunch," Mommy called as she reached for the doorknob.

"OK, I'll just run the dogs up to the creek and back," Naomi replied as she let the excited dogs out. Lucky and Bear bolted outside, each pulling in a different direction to sniff what they thought was important.

"Lucky, come!" Naomi called. Lucky strained at her harness, until she had pulled Bear away from what he was sniffing.

"Good girl! Let's go!" Naomi and the dogs went out onto the road. "Hup-up!"

Lucky leaned into her harness. Bear trotted along slightly behind Lucky's shoulders.

"Bear, why don't you help Lucky out a little and pull?" Naomi asked. "Bear, hup-up!"

For a few minutes Bear did his share of the pulling, and then he once again dropped back and let Lucky do the work. *Oh well*, Naomi thought, *Bear is a little more of a slender build than Lucky. I guess it is harder for him to pull.*

When they returned to the house, lunch was on the table.

"Time to eat!" Mommy called.

"Lucky, go lay down," Naomi commanded. Lucky obediently went into the living room and lay down. "Mmm, it sure looks good! I love having tomato sandwiches, especially when there is homemade bread!" Naomi said.

Mommy smiled. "Yes, I like it, too. Let's pray."

After the family thanked God for the food, everyone settled down to enjoy the tasty sandwiches.

"Would anyone like to float down the river after lunch? It is really hot today," Naomi said as she reached for a piece of bread.

"Well, if you kids do go, I want you to wait at least an hour. I don't want any of you to get a cramp," Mommy said.

"OK, we'll wait. It should be hotter in a few hours anyway," Naomi said.

Naomi had almost finished her second sandwich when she took the last bit of her bread and slipped it under the edge of her plate.

"Naomi! I saw that!" Mommy said, smiling. "Lucky doesn't have to have a goodie after *every* meal. She gets her own food."

Naomi lowered her eyes to her plate. "I know, but she really likes it, and she isn't begging at the table! I give it to her after we are all done."

Mommy didn't say anything else, so Naomi posed her original question to her siblings. "Do you guys want to float down the river with Lucky and me?"

"Yeah, I would like to go," Joseph said.

"Me, too!" chimed in Sarah. "That will be fun!"

An hour or so later, the children had gathered their supplies for floating down the river. They had an old logging truck inner tube, life jackets, snorkel, goggles, and fins.

"Let's go!" Naomi said as she bounced out the door into the hot sun. Joseph was putting the bicycle pump away. "Was the tube very flat?" she asked.

"No, it wasn't too bad. It only has a few slow leaks in it."

Sarah's eyes widened. "It really has leaks in it? Do you think we should even use it?"

Joseph smiled. "Everything will be fine just as long as all of us don't ride on it at once!"

"I don't mind swimming!" Naomi cried. "I'll get to use the goggles and fins!"

"I can be the first to swim behind. When I get tired, Sarah, I will switch with you." Joseph picked up the inner tube and balanced it on his head. He was wearing a wide brimmed hat that protected his face from the hot sun. Sarah picked up the life jackets, goggles, and fins and began to walk into the field behind Joseph.

"Lucky, do you want to go to the river and go for a swim?" Naomi asked. Lucky did a little dance and then ran toward the river. Mommy was standing in the doorway.

"Are you taking Lucky with you? She might not be able to keep up."

"I'll watch her. If she starts having problems, I'll walk back with her, but I think she'll be able to keep up just fine."

Lucky bumped Naomi's hand and then ran after the receding figures. Naomi ran to catch up.

"Make sure you stay close to Joseph and Sarah when you are in the water!" Mommy called after her.

"I will!" Naomi yelled over her shoulder. The feel of the grass in the field felt so good under her bare feet. When they entered the woods that bordered the river, the soft hemlock and spruce needles tickled her toes. Naomi stooped to pick some deer clover, which the children called sour grass. Sometimes they would have competitions to see who could chew the most sour grass without making a grimace at how sour it was.

"Come on, Naomi!" Joseph called.

She hurriedly clamored over a huge rotting log that lay across the trail. "I'm coming! I just had to pick a little sour grass for everyone!"

"Well, hurry and put your fins on!" Joseph was already wading out into the river. Naomi sat down on a big rock and pulled the fins onto her feet. It was hard reaching her feet with the life jacket on.

When they were all in the center of the river, Joseph carefully set the inner tube in the water. "OK, Sarah, go ahead and sit down in the inner tube." Sarah lowered herself into the inner tube, and Joseph squeezed in next to her.

"Away we go!" Joseph yelled as he lifted his feet off the river bottom and let the current carry the inner tube downstream. Naomi clung to the edge of the tube and explored the bottom of the river as it hurried beneath her. Lucky ran along the bank and looked out at the children with a worried expression on her face. She didn't like them out there, especially since her girl was in the water! At times the river slowed and it was easy for the dog to keep up. But when the river became shallow again, the water picked up its pace. After a while, Joseph wanted to swim, so Naomi and he switched places.

"Mmm, the sun sure is warm isn't it?" Naomi commented to Sarah. A deer fly buzzed around their heads. The river had slowed again. Naomi glanced shoreward. Lucky was standing on a rock, her eyes pleading for permission to come to her. "I think I'll call Lucky out to us. The water is calm for a good stretch here, so it shouldn't be too hard for her."

Naomi looked again toward the shore. "Lucky, come!" she called.

Lucky didn't need a second invitation. She leaped into the water and determinedly swam toward the floating children. "Good girl, Lucky!" Lucky swam even faster. As soon as she had reached the inner tube, she put her front feet on it and tried to pull herself up.

"Hey! What is she doing?" Sarah said.

Naomi giggled. "I think she is planning to ride the rest of the way in style! Come on, help me pull her up." After a little maneuvering, Lucky was happily seated on top of Sarah and Naomi. "You silly dog! You probably had it all planned out, didn't you?" Naomi said.

Lucky licked her face. "Watch it! Just because I'm letting you sit on me doesn't mean you can wash my face!" Naomi laughed.

For the rest of the river float, Lucky perched proudly on top of the girls. Even when they had to maneuver through some rapids, Lucky laid stoutly where she had always wanted to be—near the one she loved.

Chapter 13

Fly Spray and Show Sheen

~~~~~~~~~~~~~~~~~~

"Lucky! I can't believe it is already time for the fair! This year has gone so fast!"

Lucky tried her best to respond to Naomi's enthusiasm, but it was so hard when she was in the bathtub with smelly soap all over her. "I'm going to put some horse show sheen on your coat after your bath! That will make it even more smooth and shiny than it already is!"

Lucky's head dropped a little lower. "Don't worry, Lucky!" Naomi laughed. "It doesn't smell *that* bad!"

Soon, all the bubbles were rinsed out of the dog's beautiful coat. Lucky looked pleadingly at Naomi. "OK, you can get out of the tub now!" The dog jumped out of the tub, and quickly went out the back door. She shook and wiggled and rolled in the grass.

Naomi followed her outside. "There, do you feel better now?" she asked.

Lucky looked up at her and wiggled her answer. "Well you go ahead and have fun while I run out to the barn to find that show sheen."

Naomi skipped out to the barn. "Let's see, which one

of these is the right stuff," Naomi mumbled to herself. "I know I put show sheen and fly spray in similar bottles the other day." Unscrewing both lids, she sniffed each one. Just then Lucky pushed in beside her. "Here, Lucky, maybe you can tell, smell these and tell me which one is the show sheen," Naomi said as she pushed the open bottles under the dog's nose. "What do you think?"

Lucky's nose wrinkled up at the strange smell. "Oh, come on, Lucky, it doesn't smell that bad, does it?" Lucky backed up a few feet, her nose and eyes still scrunched up, and then she sneezed. "So that is what you think of this stuff, do you?" Naomi laughed. "But that still doesn't help me know for sure which one is the right bottle. I guess I'll have to make an educated guess." Naomi sniffed each one again. "I'm going to say it is this one. It smells a little more like show sheen than fly spray … I think."

After brushing the show sheen into Lucky's coat, Naomi carefully re-checked all the items they needed at the fair, such as the dogs' leashes, combs, toe nail clippers, ear cleaning supplies, a few dog toys and treats, dog dishes, and dog food.

Eight o'clock the next morning found them an hour away at the Port Angeles County Fairgrounds. The clamor of dogs barking and horses neighing greeted Naomi's ears. She loved the county fair. Mommy, Joseph, and Naomi with Bear and Lucky in tow made their way quickly to the small dog barn and joined the line of children with their dogs. Joseph and Naomi took their place at the back of the line. When they reached the front, a veterinarian carefully examined each dog. Bear wagged his tail and licked the lady's hand. The vet looked in his ears, felt all over the dog, and examined his coat.

It was Lucky's turn next. As the vet worked her hands

through Lucky's coat, she paused and looked at Naomi. "Did you put something in your dog's coat?" she asked. Naomi nodded. The lady continued, "Well, it is making her all sticky. You had better wash it out before you take her into the ring."

"OK," Naomi replied. Her face blushed red as she led Lucky into the barn.

"What is the matter, Naomi?" Mommy asked when she noticed the girl's red face.

"I think I accidentally put fly spray in Lucky's coat instead of show sheen!" Naomi cried.

Mommy stooped down and ran her fingers through the dog's coat. "Yes, I'm afraid you are right. You had better take her back outside and try and rinse some of it out before you have to go into the ring."

"But I have to be in the ring in 30 minutes! How will I be able to get her dry before show time?" Naomi exclaimed.

"I'll help you. You go out and rinse her off, and I'll ask Jeanne if she happens to have any dog towels we can use."

"OK," Naomi said weakly as she led Lucky outside.

The girl found a garden hose and carefully wetted Lucky's coat again. The dog licked Naomi's hand. "I'm sorry to put you through this again, doggie. I should have been more careful. Well, even if we don't win, at least no flies should bother you! We'll just think about that instead of worrying about winning. Sound like a good plan, Lucky?"

Lucky looked up at Naomi and wiggled all over. "Good girl! That's what we'll do!"

By that time, Mommy had arrived with a few towels.

"Let Lucky shake out as much water as she can, then we'll rub her dry with these towels," Mommy said.

Lucky shook herself several times and did a happy dance. She was all brushed and fluffy again by the time they had to go into the ring.

The first two days of fair flew by, and soon it was Friday afternoon. The children gathered their gear together and took the dogs off the show bench.

"I'll see you on Sunday," said Jeanne. "Oh, look at these little signs I made to put in your dog's space while you are gone tomorrow."

The sign said "Gone to Church" and was hung over a little toy dog's neck.

"That is so cute! I like it," Naomi giggled.

"It will stay right here the whole time you are gone."

As the family climbed into the van to go home, Mommy said, "Isn't that wonderful? What a witness that will be all day tomorrow."

"I'm so glad God made the Sabbath," sighed Naomi. "It will be good to rest and give Bear and Lucky a much needed break from all the stress of the fair. They will be all refreshed by Sunday."

"We all will," laughed Mommy.

That night the family had family worship to welcome in the Sabbath. Naomi always enjoyed the special time her family spent together on Friday night and Sabbath. And she loved going to Sabbath School and church. The day flew by, and before she knew it was Sunday morning and they were driving to the fairgrounds.

The last day of the fair went quickly. Naomi and Joseph had a little free time, so they wandered around to the other barns and checked out the other animals. Naomi loved walking slowly down the sawdust-covered walkway of the horse barns and peering into each stall. Some of the horses were friendly and would stand as close as they could to the bars of the door so people could scratch them between the ears. Other horses stood at the far end of their box stall and dozed.

After looking at the horses, they visited the goat and sheep barn, chicken barn, and pig barn. In the pig barn, they found a big sow with a litter of fat, pink piglets.

Joseph's favorite barn was the draft horse barn. The horses there were calm and docile, but they made the people working with them seem very small.

After getting a good look around, they hurried back to the dog barn to get ready for the agility competition, which was always fun. The dogs ran through a course of jumps, tunnels, and high walkways. Bear flew over the jumps as if he was a bird. Lucky enjoyed it too, but she was a little slower than Bear. There was also the brace competition where two dogs did the heeling exercises with one person. Lucky and Bear made a good team, even when Lucky insisted on being closest to Naomi throughout the whole exercise.

Then there was the team obedience test in which four handler and dog teams did the heeling pattern together. Everyone had to be careful to walk the same speed and to stop at the same time. It was a fun challenge. After the last competition, everyone waited for the results to be announced.

Once the judges scored had been tabulated, everyone was called out into the ring. The barn supervisor held a microphone and a large clipboard in her hand. "Can I have everyone's attention please? I am now going to read off the names of those who qualified to go to the state fair in Puyallup. Everyone please be quiet until all the names are read."

Naomi held her breath. *Will Lucky qualify for the state fair? We did really well in obedience, but I know our scores in fitting and showing weren't the best. Lucky is still having a hard time standing still while the judge examines her. I guess I'll know in a minute.*

Naomi jerked back to the present as she heard the woman announce, "Naomi Cowles and Lucky."

We're going! We made it! In a few months we will be going to the big city to compete! Naomi wanted to run into the barn and give Lucky a big hug, but instead she closed her eyes and thanked Jesus for helping Lucky do so well.

Chapter 14

The Wonderful Pest

~~~~~~~~~~~~~~~

It was 6:00 a.m. on a clear cool morning as Naomi followed the path leading to the barn. She breathed in the fresh morning air. Pausing for a moment, she closed her eyes and listened to a robin sing a sleepy good morning to the world.

Caw, caw, caw! Opening her eyes again, Naomi looked up into the sky. A lone crow was flying toward her. "Here, Mo! Come on you rascal!" Naomi called as she lifted her hand above her head. The crow folded his wings and dived toward her. As he neared, he spread his wings again to slow down and then lighted on her upraised hand. "You silly bird! Did you go to town again this morning? The old farm isn't exciting enough for you anymore, huh?"

Mo side-stepped his way up Naomi's arm until he was on her shoulder. The bird cuddled up to Naomi's neck and made a soft low noise. "Are you needing a good head scratch, Mo? Here you go. I can't scratch long because it is my turn to milk Daisy this morning. I can't be late!"

After a moment, Naomi reached down for the empty milk pail. Lucky was already waiting by the barn door. "Come on, Mo, you can help too!" After closing the door behind them, she placed the milk pail on a stand near the stanchion. Mo flew from her shoulder to the wooden divider that separated the goat pen from the milk stanchion. Naomi reached into a red bin for a scoop of grain and poured it into Daisy's pan. Mo marched back and forth on the divider and eyed the wonderful grain he wasn't supposed to have.

"Mo! Don't even think about it! You know that grain is for the goat, not you! Here, have some of your own." Naomi reached into her pocket and brought out some spare grain and held it out to the crow. Mo greedily grabbed the biggest piece of corn and gobbled it down. "There, now you stay away from Daisy's breakfast!"

Naomi opened the gate for the waiting goat. Daisy ran and jumped up onto the stanchion and stuck her head through the hole to reach the grain. Soon the warm milk was zinging into the pail. *I love the smell of milk and the feel of Daisy's warm side. It is all so peaceful,* Naomi thought. She glanced over her shoulder to see Lucky patiently lying down with her head resting on her paws. Mo was still pacing back and forth on the divider.

Naomi closed her eyes and leaned up against Daisy a little more, enjoying the quiet of the morning. But suddenly there was a flurry of wings, a snort, and a sharp kick. "DAISY! What did you do that for!" Naomi righted the milk pail again. "It was almost half full!"

Naomi stood up and looked around. Her eyes rested on Mo with a mouthful a grain. "Mo! Did you just steal that from Daisy? Shame on you! Lucky, get that troublemaker out of here!" Naomi commanded. Lucky jumped to her feet and barked at the crow. Mo, seeing that he was outnumbered, quickly flew out the horse door in search of more trouble. "It's alright, Daisy. The crow is gone now, so finish your breakfast."

When the milking was done, Naomi turned the goats out into their pen. Then she picked up the pail of milk and went to the house. In the kitchen Naomi found the milk strainer. She carefully poured the fresh milk through the strainer into a clean half-gallon jar. She then quickly put the jar in a plastic tub with ice water. With a long handled spoon, she stirred the milk. Several times she put a thermometer in the milk to see how cool it was. By breakfast time the milk had cooled sufficiently to be put into the refrigerator. If the milk was put away without cooling it first, it would age much faster than normal.

As they ate breakfast, Naomi told her family about how Mo had "helped" her with the milking. "That crow's middle name should be trouble!" Mom said. "That seems to be his favorite occupation, seeing what mischief he can find! The other day as I was picking strawberries in the garden he flew in and stole berries out of my bowl! After I chased him away, he went to the tomatoes and started pecking holes in all the red ones!"

Daddy smiled. "Yes, he is a little pest at times, but I'm happy that he is free to come and go as he likes, and years later when he leaves to live with his kind, we'll look back on these memories with a smile."

Naomi had found Mo in the woods when he was just a little guy. She had brought him to the house and put him in a cage with a cardboard box lined with hay and some of Lucky's soft fur. Mo seemed happy with his new arrangements, for when he cuddled down into the warm fur, he fell fast asleep.

Over the next few weeks, Naomi gained a new respect for parent birds. She understood now why in the summer they always seemed to be in such a hurry. Mo kept Naomi busy all day long. First thing in the morning Mo squawked for food. Naomi would stick boiled egg down his throat and then hurry out to do the morning chores. When she walked in the back door, Mo would be calling again for more food. Then after her own breakfast and family worship, Mo would be hungry again! After feeding him, she had to wipe his mouth and throat with a damp paper towel to clean off the food that hadn't made it inside. If the food wasn't cleaned off right away, it would harden on his tender skin and cause sores. After cleaning him, Naomi then had to change his bedding. In a couple of hours, he was again calling for more food.

Even though it was a lot of work, it was also very rewarding for Naomi. After a few weeks of this constant business, Mo was ready to move outside. He had grown amazingly fast and was now covered in a handsome black coat. He still had some baby fuzz sticking out from his head like little antennas, and his mouth was still big and yellow, but he had outgrown his cage and was eager for adventure.

One warm sunny morning, Naomi took Mo outside for the first time. Mo crouched down and leaned up against Naomi's neck. "It's OK, Mo! You are safe here. Don't be afraid." Naomi put her hand up to Mo, and the crow stepped onto it. His little black claws dug into her hand. "There, there, little guy, don't be afraid," Naomi crooned.

Mo crouched again on her hand and then sidestepped up her arm until he was pressed against her neck once more. "You might be a little scared now, but soon you will love it out here. For now you can ride on my shoulder, and I will give you a grand tour of the farm."

Mo quickly learned to love the outside world. Every morning he clamored to get out and play. He always tagged along with Naomi at chore time, and he followed the family wherever they went outside. In the evenings he would fly into the back porch and roost on a wooden peg.

Now Mo was a permanent resident at the farm. He was often a pest, but Naomi loved him just the same. One morning as Naomi was practicing the recall exercise with Lucky, Mo flew in to see what they were doing. He landed on top of the house and cocked his head with a saucy look as he watched the proceedings below.

Naomi called to the bird, "Mo, you had better mind your manners. Lucky and I don't have time for any monkey business right now. We are practicing for the state fair, so you just watch from up there." Mo ruffled his feathers and began to strut around as if to say, "Me? You think I would cause trouble?"

"Alright, Lucky, let's do one more recall," Naomi said. "Lucky sit."

Lucky sat squarely in front of Naomi, her eyes fixed on Naomi's face.

"Lucky, stay." Turning quickly, Naomi walked across the lawn, and then she turned again to face the dog. Lucky leaned forward, ready to leap into action as soon as Naomi gave the word.

"Lucky, come!" The dog ran full speed ahead and slid into a sitting position at Naomi's feet.

"Good girl, Lucky. Go get the ball!"

Naomi threw the ball. It sailed through the air, and Lucky bounded after it. All of a sudden something black dove down from the roof and landed next to the ball.

"Mo! I told you to mind your manners!" Naomi scolded. But Mo had no intention of minding his manners. He opened his beak wide and tried to pick up the tennis ball, but it was too heavy for him, so he straddled it, looked at the confused dog, and made a funny little noise like a dog's growl.

"Mo, you give that ball to Lucky right now. I threw it for her, not you! You only want it because she does!" Lucky lay down and poked her nose toward the ball. The crow growled even more fiercely and flapped his wings. Lucky looked at Naomi.

"Mo, that is enough of this foolishness," Naomi said as she picked up the protesting bird. "Here, take this piece of corn, and go hide it somewhere, but leave Lucky's ball alone!"

Mo greedily grabbed the peace offering and flew away toward one of his many stashes where he hid his loot. "Crazy bird," Naomi muttered under her breath in mock disgust.

Chapter 15

A Farm Girl's Champion

~~~~~~~~~~~~~~~~

The sound of dogs barking and people talking greeted Naomi and her family as they entered the dog barn at the state fair. Naomi trembled with excitement as she helped Lucky up to her assigned bench. Several other club members had also qualified for the Washington State Fair and were already getting their dogs ready for the first show.

Lucky

Jeanne greeted them and gave them a schedule of the different dog classes. "Naomi, you and Joseph will have your fitting and showing class in about an hour. Do you feel ready?"

"I'm as ready as I'll ever be," Naomi said with a nervous smile.

"Well, I'm sure you will do well. Just stay calm and focus on helping Lucky do her best," Jeanne advised.

"OK, I'll try. It's hard to believe I'm actually here! I've studied the questions for weeks. I hope I don't miss any! They are all jumbled up in my head now!"

"Don't worry," Jeanne said. "You've studied hard, and you've worked with Lucky a lot. Just try and relax, and do your best and have fun!"

Before Naomi realized it, it was time to enter the ring. Lucky was so clean and shining that no one would have guessed that she was a farm dog. Her white collar was as white as could be. There wasn't a piece of hair out of place. Her ears were so clean that not the least bit of dirt or earwax could be found, and her feet were beautiful.

"Lucky, here we go. Let's do our best and have fun," Naomi whispered to Lucky as the class began to file into the ring.

The line of children with their dogs circled the ring at a fast pace. Then they lined up as the judge walked up and down the line, looking at each pair. Naomi carefully positioned Lucky's feet so she would be standing squarely, and then she waited as the judge looked Lucky up and down.

After the judge had looked at all of the dogs in line, she called the first dog to come to her in the middle of the ring. The judge then examined the dog to see how well it was groomed. She asked the handler a few questions; then she watched as the handler and dog ran down to the end of the ring and back.

"They did really good, Lucky, don't you think?" Naomi whispered to Lucky.

Soon Naomi and Lucky were walking to the center of the ring for their turn with the judge. *Dear Jesus, please help us to remember what we have learned and do our best,* Naomi prayed.

The woman watched as Naomi repositioned Lucky's feet again. Then the judge felt Lucky all over and looked in her ears and mouth. Lucky stood calmly. Naomi breathed a sigh of relief.

"You have a very nice dog," she said to Naomi. "Now, I have a few questions to ask you. Where did your dog's breed originate?"

Naomi swallowed hard and said, "The Australian Shepherd originated in the United States."

The judge looked at her clipboard and said, "What act by Congress established 4-H club work?"

Naomi answered, "Congress established the 4-H club work in an act called the Smith Lever Act."

The judge looked at her clipboard again. "Give three symptoms of distemper."

Naomi took a deep breath and said, "Loss of appetite, eye and nose discharge, convulsions."

The judge smiled and asked, "What is the difference between natural and acquired immunity?"

Naomi shut her eyes tight and stroked Lucky's head. "Um, the difference between natural and acquired immunity is ... um ... natural immunity means that an animal cannot get sick. I mean, the animal is not able to catch the disease, and acquired immunity is when the animal has developed antibodies to that disease."

The judge looked at Naomi and said, "Please show me where the sternum is on your dog."

Naomi quickly pointed to Lucky's sternum, and then the judge said, "Please take your dog down and back for me."

Naomi led Lucky to the starting point and then trotted

Lucky down to the end of the ring and back. When they got back to the starting point, the judge said, "OK, take your dog back to the lineup."

Naomi smiled and led Lucky in a fast trot to the end of the line. "Phew," Naomi confided in Lucky. "She asked me some hard questions. I hope I got them right. You did really good, puppy," Naomi said as she carefully placed Lucky's feet where she wanted them.

After the judge had examined every dog and questioned every handler, she took her clipboard over to the ring steward, and they quickly added up the points everyone had received. Then the judge walked back into the ring carrying a box full of ribbons. Someone gave her a microphone so the handlers and the spectators could hear her.

"This is a very impressive group of competitors. They all did very well. They knew their 4-H questions, and their dogs were all well groomed. I just want to say that I am very proud of all of you. You are all winners already. It was a challenge picking the one to take home the champion ribbon today."

The judge began to read off arm numbers and hand out ribbons. Most everyone received a blue ribbon. Soon the ones who had placed were being called. Fourth place. Third place. Second place. Naomi held her breath. They were about to name the grand champion.

"Number 112 receives Reserve Grand Champion," the judge called.

Naomi gave Lucky a quick hug. "That's us, girl. You did so good!"

They trotted toward the judge, accepted their ribbon, and returned to their place in line. The ribbon was light purple with a big rosette that had the words "Puyallup State Fair, Reserve Grand Champion of Fitting and

Showing" printed on it.

Naomi smiled and prayed silently. *Thank you, Jesus, for helping us. Thank you for helping me to do my best, and Lucky too.*

Then she turned to her dog. "Here, Lucky, you take it. This is really your ribbon," Naomi said. She handed the ribbon to Lucky. The dog took the big ribbon and held it proudly.

"We have only two hours until the obedience competition. That has always been much more enjoyable to us. We should go rest until then, and I'll give you a treat for getting this ribbon!"

"Good job!" Mommy said as they came out of the ring. What an honor to get such an award in such a tough competition."

"Yes, Lucky did great. She did so well holding still and letting the judge look at her," Naomi replied. "Now we just have open obedience in two hours! That will be fun!"

Naomi and Lucky sat and rested while they waited for their time in the obedience ring. *Obedience is always more fun than fitting and showing,* she thought to herself. *I prefer it to just standing in a line and then running in circles. Lucky gets to retrieve stuff and do scent discrimination and recalls! Even if we don't place high, it is more fun because it is like we are just playing with each other.*

The next thing Naomi knew Mommy was shaking her. "Wake up! You have just a few minutes until you go into the ring again."

Naomi stood up and rubbed her eyes. "OK," she mumbled.

Taking Lucky off the bench, she took her out to the potty area so Lucky could relieve herself. After that was done, Naomi gathered together the articles she would need in the ring. The leash, scent articles, gloves for the directed retrieve, and Lucky's dumbbell.

As she waited her turn to enter the ring, Naomi prayed again. *Dear Jesus, here we go again. Thank you for helping us so much already. Please be with us as we do these obedience exercises. Help me to stay relaxed and focus on giving Lucky clear commands. And help Lucky to not get distracted and to remember what we have been practicing. Thank you, amen.*

"Number 112!" the ring steward called. Naomi handed the articles to the steward and went into the ring.

"You may remove the leash," the judge said. Naomi unsnapped the leash from Lucky's collar.

"This is the heeling exercise. Are you ready?" the judge asked.

Naomi looked down at Lucky sitting at her side. "Yes," she stated.

"Forward," the judge said.

Naomi looked at Lucky again and said in a happy voice. "Lucky, heel!"

Lucky pranced by her side. They stopped, turned, and walked fast and slow as the judge told them to do so.

"Exercise finished," the judge finally said.

They did the retrieve test next. Naomi threw the dumbbell to the other side of the ring. When the judge gave the signal, Naomi said, "Lucky, take it!" Lucky bounded to the dumbbell, picked it up, and brought it back. Then they did the same retrieve but this time over a jump.

The judge wrote something down on her clipboard. "Alright, now we will do the directed retrieve."

The steward brought out three white gloves. She placed each one in a different location in the ring. The judge nodded to the ring steward, and then she turned to

Naomi. "This is the directed retrieve, are you ready?"

"Yes," Naomi said, and Lucky turned to face the glove that the judge specified.

"Send your dog."

Lucky tensed as she waited for the command. "Lucky, take it!" Naomi said. Lucky quickly retrieved the correct glove.

The rest of the exercises went smoothly as well. As soon as they had finished the last one, Naomi leaned over and gave Lucky a big hug. "Good girl, Lucky. You did so well!"

When the scores were added up, the competitors were called back into the ring. As Naomi waited for her number to be called, she thought to herself. *It doesn't really matter what the judge decides. I know that Lucky is the best dog in the world! Not just because she did so well today, but because Jesus gave her to me. And no matter what ribbon we get, I know I will be proud of her.*

Once again, her thoughts were interrupted by the judge's voice.

"Number 112!"

Naomi looked up. The steward was holding a large purple ribbon and a small silver trophy. "Number 112 receives the Grand Champion ribbon."

Naomi's eyes grew wide, and a shiver of happiness ran up and down her spine. She couldn't move for a moment, and then Lucky pressed her cold nose into her hand, as if to say, "Come on; let's go get our prize!"

Naomi carefully fingered the big ribbon and trophy that the steward handed her. Her eyes became misty. *Thank you, Jesus, for answering my prayer those many years ago. You have given me a better dog than I could have ever imagined. Lucky has taught me so many things and is such a good friend. Thank you so much for giving me Lucky.*

We invite you to view the complete
selection of titles we publish at:

www.TEACHServices.com

Scan with your mobile
device to go directly
to our website.

Please write or e-mail us your praises, reactions, or
thoughts about this or any other book we publish at:

TEACH Services, Inc.
P U B L I S H I N G
www.TEACHServices.com • (800) 367-1844

P.O. Box 954
Ringgold, GA 30736

info@TEACHServices.com

TEACH Services, Inc., titles may be purchased in bulk for
educational, business, fund-raising, or sales promotional use.
For information, please e-mail:

BulkSales@TEACHServices.com

Finally, if you are interested in seeing
your own book in print, please contact us at

publishing@TEACHServices.com

We would be happy to review your manuscript for free.

CPSIA information can be obtained
at www.ICGtesting.com
Printed in the USA
FSOW01n0431270215
5382FS